ANGLER'S GUIDE TO
BAJA
CALIFORNIA

ED TABOR

BY TOM MILLER

Baja Trail Publications, Inc.
Huntington Beach, California

Acknowledgements

As I get deeper into the writing profession, I have reached the conclusion that the easiest part of writing a book is to come up with the original idea. Next comes the question of marketing and whether the knowledge needed to present a complete and responsible picture to the hoped-for reader is available.

As new ideas tumble over old, the initial outline is followed by many revisions, and reams of paper go under the typewriter roller and out onto the floor.

When the manuscript finally takes shape, one finds that it has taken many people to nurture that original idea before it is ready for the printer. To those whom I owe so much, I extend my deepest appreciation:

To Shirley Miller, a master at organizing, editing and typing the final manuscript.

To Mike Glover, who has created another winner with his excellent cover design.

To the people of the State of California Department of Fish and Game for their generosity in allowing me to use some of their fish identification drawings. The balance came from the pen of Charles Larson, one of the finest artists I know.

To others who have provided invaluable assistance and information: Bill Beebe, Bill Bellinger, Cindy Casey, Harry Kime, Jerry Klink, Frank Lo Preste, Leonard Lussier, Chuck Miller, Dan Miller, Si Nathanson, John Perkins, Joe Pfister, Tony Reyes, Jack Ridenoure, Bob Taft, Al Tetzlaff, Pat Trainor, Burt Twilegar and A. A. Wilson.

And to a long list of other people who over the years have also contributed -- the Baja fishermen, the skippers, the resort managers and the inhabitants of the peninsula's many fishing camps.

My special thanks to all.

Tom Miller

ANGLER'S GUIDE TO BAJA CALIFORNIA . . . Published by Baja Trail Publications, Inc., P.O. Box 6088, Huntington Beach, CA 92615. ISBN 0–914622-04-8.

Dedication

Thirty years ago, Ray Cannon took literally the advice of his physician to "get out of Los Angeles," so he headed for Baja California to fish himself back to health. He did that and more.

Cannon, a name linked with the movie greats of the silent era as an actor, director and writer, began a new career that charged the fishing world with a euphoria that will continue throughout many lifetimes.

Ray's infectuous enthusiasm about Baja fishing has been reflected in his many articles and his classic book, *The Sea of Cortez*. It is unlikely that most of us would have ventured into Baja California were it not for this man.

Although his love affair with Baja ended officially in June of 1977 with his passing, we know that it continues, for Ray's ashes are scattered in his beloved Sea of Cortez. Each airport, hotel and resort remains as a monument to his vision.

With love and affection, I dedicate this book to the memory of Ray Cannon.

Tom Miller
April, 1979

Foreword

In the decade since Tom Miller first began to write for **Western Outdoor News,** he has attracted a large following among the growing throngs who fly and drive to Mexico. His love for isolated beaches, "tight lines" and the companionship of scattered ranchers and fishermen, has led him to explore almost every part of the more than 2,000 miles of shoreline on the Baja California peninsula.

In the tradition of his colleague, the late Ray Cannon, Miller has shared his considerable knowledge through his writings. His book, **The Baja Book II**, co-authored with Elmar Baxter, proved to be one of the most popular ever written for the Baja traveler; and it is my belief that this book, **Angler's Guide to Baja California**, will lead more thousands to explore the seas and beaches of our neighbor to the South.

Burt Twilegar, President
Western Outdoors Publications, Inc.

Contents

Acknowledgements 2
Dedication 3
Foreword 4
Introduction 7
    Giant Grouper Dilemma 8
The Three Angles of Baja 9
Getting It Together 10
    Baja Tackle 10
    Long-Range Tackle 13
Jig Fishing 14
Baits 16
Flyfishing 17
One Step from Immortality 18
Baja's Fishing Zones 19
Zone I: North Pacific Coast 22
    Los Coronados 24
    A Place to Watch 25
    A Highly Visitable Spot 26
    Perch—Big And Plenty 27
    Surf Fishing Paradise 28
    The First Long-Range Trip 29
    A World To Itself 30
Zone II: Central Portion 32
    The Honey Pot 34
    Abreojos—An Eye Opener 35
Zone III: Magdalena Bay 36
    Snook Country 38
Zone IV: Cabo—The Cape 40
    Those Glamour Fish 42
    The Wahoo Banks 43
Zone V: The East Cape 44
    Frustration At Frailes 46
    Pez Gallo 47
    Fisherman's Point 48
    Punta Arena De La Ventana 49
    The Remote Cerralvo 50
Zone VI: La Paz 52
    Yellowfin—Yellowtail 54
    Tuna By The Mile 55
Zone VII: Loreto-Mulege 56
    Only By Boat 58
    A Winter Haven 59
    The Lure of Loreto 60
    A Popular Bay 61
    Sierra—The Cebiche Fish 62
    Lesson At Mulege 63

Zone VIII: The Cortez Midriff 64
    Yellowtail Alley 66
    Viva Papa, Viva Mama 67
    Refugio 68
Zone IX: The North Cortez 70
    End Of A Long Trail 72
    Croaker Country 73
Zone X: The Revillagigedo Archipelago 74
What Is It? 76
    Sharks And Rays 77
    Silvery Fishes 81
    Elongated Fishes 82
    Bottom Dwellers 83
    Basses 84
    Dorado, Mackerels And Tunas 88
    Jacks 90
    Corvinas And Croakers 93
    Surf Fishes 96
    Billfishes 98
    Flat Fishes 100
    Wrasses and Parrotfishes 100
    Snappers 101
    Miscellaneous and Oddballs 103
When Are They There? 106
Baja Fishing Calendars 106
    Needlefish 117
    Man With A Plan 117
Supplemental Reading and Special Trips 118
Fishing Spanish 119
Resorts 121
A World of Records 123
Mexican Fishing Regulations 124
A Resource-Full Sea 125
Huachinango Express 126

Introduction

It is hard to imagine that less than a generation ago the name, Baja California, meant little except to those who lived near the border and a select few adventuresome anglers. It was then that tales began drifting north about the fishing along the more than 2000 miles of coast line.

The capture of marlin from dugout canoes, yellowtail striking the lures of shorecasters, totuava topping 200 pounds, and thousands of variations of these themes, caused fishermen over the years to head for the atlas on the bookshelf. It sounded like their kind of place.

Those who found that long finger of rocks, desert and beaches, and pursued the stories, discovered that in Baja the license of exaggeration given fishermen rarely needed to be used. The action was there.

Twenty years ago, half-a-dozen angler-oriented hotels were scattered from Mulegé to Cabo San Lucas and 99% of the clientele arrived by air. Paved roads extended only to San Felipe and about 50 miles below Ensenada. It took seven days of hard driving to make it from Tijuana to La Paz...if your car would hold together. The intervening 800 miles was really bad. There were so few people that the entire population of Baja south of Ensenada could sit comfortably in Dodger Stadium.

Then, in the late sixties, the siren's call of this shimmering peninsula caught the imagination of the television industry. Bing Crosby sang songs of the sea while he battled a sailfish for the cameras of the American Broadcasting Company; "The Baja 1000" attracted millions of network viewers; Cousteau intrigued us with the life story of the California gray whale; and, of course, there were those recurring stories of the fishing.

With the completion of the paved transpeninsula highway, Mexico 1, in late 1973, fully 25 hotels, motels and RV parks were ready to accommodate the new visitors. Today the number approaches 40 with more on the drawing board.

The purpose of this book is to bring to the American angler an insight of where, when and how to fish the seas that surround the Baja California peninsula—in short, to impart a "local knowledge." The information comes from the author's personal experiences of nearly 30 years, plus interviews with hundreds of anglers who too have felt the exhilaration of tight lines, bent rods and singing reels under the Baja sun.

Today the fishing quality in the waters of the Pacific Ocean and Sea of Cortez touching Baja is unequaled anywhere in the Americas. Hundreds of species of gamefish are there to be challenged with sporting tackle ranging from 80 pound "monster rigs" to whippy ultra-light outfits and the increasingly popular saltwater flyrod.

Baja is one of the few remaining places where the fishing of the "good old days" still exists and, with care and conservation, will be around for our great grandchildren.

Giant Grouper Dilemma

Mycteroperca jordani might be considered by many people as the medical term for a hernia. In icthyological circles the moniker belongs to the *baya* or gulf grouper.

He is the best friend a tackle store could ask for. Whole yellowtail, with attached 8/0 to 12/0 hooks disappear into his mouth like popcorn at a western movie. Over a grouper hole, the cry, "Hook up!" followed by "#$¢*, son of a @$&*!" is the order of the day. But should you heft that grouper into the boat you'll have some of the best-eating fillets the sea has to offer.

The grouper, even when small, is a predacious cuss, often attacking lures nearly twice his size. Many times I've thrown back little ones who were no bigger than the jig I was using. When the baya reaches about ten pounds he takes lures into the rocks before you have time to react. At times it seemed as if I were trading a pound of lead for each pound of grouper.

The rocks and subterranean caves throughout the Cortez and below Magdalena on the Pacific side are home territory for the grouper. By ingesting almost everything in sight he grows to well over 200 pounds. His modus operandi is to stay near his cave until the quarry ventures within range. Then he pounces with surprising speed and heads for the rocks. This trait often leaves the guy on the other end of the line only 10 or 15 feet in which to keep from being "rocked". Rarely does conventional tackle cut it when the fish exceeds 50 pounds. Anglers using a "broomstick" stiff rod and 130 pound test line have been almost catapulted into the water when the rod hit the gunnel.

Once, while fishing a reef off Punta Rocasa on the east side of Isla Angel de La Guarda, 12 of us in four skiffs hooked and "liberated" over 100 grouper in two days and brought only four to the gaff. The rest kept our donated equipment. On another trip to the same spot, a friend told of taking a 100 pound grouper which had a total of four jigs hanging from its mouth, including his. They were all in good shape, indicating that the fish had acquired his collection within a very short time and hadn't yet learned not to chase white pieces of metal.

If I were ever to get serious about grouper fishing again I think I would take several hundred feet of nylon parachute cord, a supply of 12/0 hooks and a pair of gloves. Then I'll tie that line to the boat's davit and hang on. I don't need a hernia.

The Three Angles of Baja

The angler who visits Baja has three basic environments in which to wet his line: offshore; inshore and onshore.

The *offshore* fishing grounds are those regions of "blue water" that are generally beyond the 100 fathom line. At times this line may be less than a mile from shore, as at Cabo San Lucas, Los Frailes and numerous places in the Midriff Islands, providing offshore conditions almost within casting distance of the beach.

The quarry is usually the pelagic populations of the billfish and tuna families, plus the dorado or dolphinfish. Most are taken by trolling, as their seasonal north-south migrations bring them past the many sub-surface seamounts which dot the Eastern Pacific and the Sea of Cortez.

Inshore fishing begins around the reefs which extend upward from about 50 fathoms and serve as a haven for the bass, grouper and the dozens of other rockdwellers. The large shoals of forage which gather over such structures also serve to attract such shallow water migrants as sierra, barracuda, white seabass, yellowtail and other members of the jack family. A wide variety of trolling, jigfishing and baitfishing techniques are employed in the inshore fishery.

The pursuit of the *onshore* fishery is, to many dedicated anglers, the most challenging of the three. Here, using little more than a good pair of legs and an eye sharpened by a close observation of the structure to determine likely habitat, the onshore angler, or surf fisherman, can combine an easy pace with a highly productive pursuit. His skills also include the gathering of natural baits, selection of artificials and the ability to cast his offering accurately.

General angling techniques and tackle selection for the three types of fishing will be covered thoroughly in the chapter titled: *Getting It Together.*

Little compares to the exhiliration of matching up with a worthy opponent.

AL TETZLAFF

TOM MILLER

Getting It Together
Baja Tackle

It is generally agreed that more than 250 species of gamefish inhabit the seas around the Baja California peninsula. Ranging from a pound to over a thousand, they all are capable of providing exciting challenges for the angler on the proper tackle. The problem comes in coming up with a correctly matched arsenal to cover all possibilities, and short of a quarter-ton arsenal of rods, reels, lures, hooks, lines, sinkers, swivels and wire, plus the amenities. Even then you are likely to come up short somewhere down the line.

If you don't choose to buy out a tackle store, you might find the following helpful in establishing guidelines:

It is not cheap to fish anywhere away from home. A trip to Baja can represent a sizeable investment, so protect that investment . . . by buying quality equipment. When in the world's finest fishing waters were record-size fish abound, it doesn't make sense to use marginal gear. If you do, you're only asking for trouble . . . shattered rods, corroded guides, frozen drags and popped lines are frustrations you don't need. In the long run the difference in cost between cheap and quality is less than you think, particularly when amortizing the cost over the life of the tackle. Watch the sales and compare values, you'll come out ahead.

For what it's worth, my current "minimum" tackle list is down to what follows, and I've found it cover about 95% of my needs when flying or driving to Baja . . .

I have narrowed down to four rods, which I carry in a sturdy rod case; one is a new, 5 to 5 1/2-foot state-of-the-art "tuna" rod designed for 30 to 40-pound line. It is used for handling surface and yo-yo jigs weighing up to 6 ounces. The second is slightly longer, and for lines in the 16 to 25-pound range. It should be able to handle live bait and small lures.

The third rod is a 8 to 9-foot 2-piece spinning rod for 16 to 30-pound line. Primarily for use from shore, it should be able to handle weights up to 4 ounces. The top foot or so of the rod is painted white, to make it more visible when night fishing.

The fourth rod is a 6-foot ultralight spinner for 4 to 8-pound line. Using small, freshwater-type lures or bait it serves well for the dozens of species found in the sandy and rocky intertidal regions of the Sea of Cortez. Once, within walking distance of Hotel Punta Colorada, I took 15 different species in one morning using white crappie feathers and pieces of shrimp.

My tackle box will usually contain a minimum of four reels — two conventional and two spinning. Of the conventionals one is capable of holding about 400 yards of 30-pound test monofilament, the other is a bit smaller and intended for 20-pound mono. Though it may seem going too light to many we have found that today it is not unusual to hear of marlin and sails being taken on 30, 20 or even 12-pound line. I and my companions have done it a number of times from small boats by working the fish hard and close to the limits of the equipment. There are fish that will be lost no matter the gear, so we don't worry about it. If you feel that you are outclassed, you can always rent heavier marlin tackle from the resorts.

Of the two spinners, one is a medium-sized saltwater variety, the other a lightweight model for use on the ultralight rod. I carry at least one extra spool for each reel.

There are a number of quality reel manufacturers from which to choose. And with new designs and spaceage materials we have a choice of the finest equipment ever. For conventional reels we suggest you consider the following: the Shimano lever drag series, TLD 10, TLD15, and the larger TLD20, or, Diawa's lever drag units, LD30H and LD50H, and the Penn 506HS and 505HS. Another very well made line of reels are from the Carl Newell Company, Glendale, CA. Their matching model numbers are P332F, P338F and P447F.

An adequate supply of well-maintained equipment is a must for the Baja angler.

For spinning spinning reels we have had good personal experiences with the Shimano deluxe line, while others recommend the Daiwa SS series.

It isn't often that I even take extra line (except for the 4 and 6 pound mono). By starting with spools, and extra spools all filled with a good quality, abrasion resistant line, I have survived several weeks of moderate to heavy fishing without running out. Ande, Berkeley, Izorline, Maxima and Stren all provide quality monofilament lines, and you'll find a wide variety of preferences among veteran Baja anglers.

You can also protect your line by regulary checking that guides are in good order (no nicks or grooves) and that the drag system smooth. If I run out of a line size, I switch to another, usually the next size smaller. Learning to meet the new, tougher challenge can lead to becoming a better fisherman.

The types and sizes of hooks, sinkers and other terminal tackle vary widely. Hooks range from small No. 8 baitholder style for the ultralight rigs (we've even used salmon-egg hooks to catch the tiniest reef species) on up to 6/0 or 9/0 O'Shaugnessy type hooks for feeding a large live bait to a marlin or roosterfish.

Heavy 80, 120 and 180-pound monofilament is included for marlin leaders. Wire in varying weights is also a must if trying for wahoo, sierra and other sharptoothed species. The Sevenstrand nylon coated leader material — the coating melts and forms a strong bond when heated with a match or lighter — does away with annoying crimp sleeves.

Twist-on, surf, torpedo egg sinkers to 4 ounces, plus small weights down to tiny split-shots, are also part of the equipment. Don't forget dark-finish swivels and rings (many fish will hit the shiny ones), long-nosed pliers, sidecutters, sharpening stone, knife and a rod-butt belt.

The Coronado Islands yield thousands of yellowtail to the San Diego party-boat passengers.

Long-Range Tackle

Boarding one of the long-range sportfishing boats and heading for the offshore reefs south of Cedros Island is like stepping into a different set of conditions than usually encountered on the Baja peninsula. The fishing is from a large boat which cannot be maneuvered to help relieve strain on light tackle with limited line capacity. Also, it is the domain of the yellowfin tuna and the wahoo.

Most experienced anglers agree that there is no stronger or more durable fish than a yellowfin tuna: after they pass the 60 pound mark, fishing tuna with a small capacity reel and light line is an exercise in futility. Therefore, when I board the boat to head into the big tuna, from Alijos Rocks to the Revillagigedo Archipelago, I juggle my tackle a bit.

I leave the very light tackle home, for it will only get in the way. For these trips I start with a spinning outfit to handle 15 to 20 pound test line, then graduate through the conventional tackle mentioned in the previous section. I bring extra line, as fishing from a dead boat provides is a greater chance of being stripped, or having the line damaged. To the above I add two short (5′ to 5′3″) rods capable of handling 50 to 80-pound line on International 50 or 50W reels. Both rods have roller guides, long foregrips and gimbaled butt piece to fit the gimbaled rod-butt belt.

Dramatic improvements in tackle design and the use of space-age materials allows today's angler to challenge even larger fish with lighter equipment. All reels are equipped with the new, lightweight aluminum spools as manufactured by both Penn and the Carl W. Newell Company. These spools are stronger than either the old brass or plastic spools which normally come with a stock reel. This allows me to jig cast with a 4/0 reel just as easilly as with the smaller Pen 500 size. On a 6/0 the advantage is greater capacity and the easier casting of heavier live baits.

Another must for tuna is a shoulder harness which attaches to the holes in the frames of the reel. This allows my arms to rest as the battle wears on.

As much of the fishing is from an anchored boat, I bring a few large sinkers weighing up to 3 pounds to counteract the current when putting a bait near the bottom.

Jig Fishing

Whether made from feathers, wood, plastic, aluminum, zinc or lead — or a combination thereof — whether trolled or cast, bounced over rocks or along the bottom, it seems that West Coast anglers tend to call all artificial saltwater lures a "jig." So that we all know what we're talking about, let's list and describe some of these jigs.

Candy Bar—is named for its shape; flat on the bottom with cylindrical top and tapered sides. It is a most versatile jig. Coming in an array of weights, profiles, sizes and colors, it can be used to take almost anything that eats live bait. Some well-known names of this family of jigs are Seastrike, Salas, Yo Ho Ho and Tady. A personal rating of the best colors for Baja are white, chrome, white-blue, white-red, green and yellow in that order, but any color may work at any one time.

Spoons or Wobblers—the big cousins of the freshwater lures; a convex-concave design lends a lot of action to the lure, even when retrieved at slow speeds. Most are used as surface lures. Examples of this type are Krocodile, Seastrike, Tady and Tony Aceta. The chrome versions are usually most effective.

Leadheads—basically a painted lead weight molded onto a long-shanked hook and dressed up with feathers, nylon and acrylic filaments, colored vinyl skirts, or even the multicolored prismatic Mylar. Trolled, cast, or bounced off the bottom leadheads attract a wide variety of fish. I consider leadheads my best all-around lure for catching table fish.

An increasingly popular form of leadhead uses a soft plastic "swimming" trailing portion. Its effectiveness is in the "tail" design, which resembles a live shrimp or baitfish. Though the tails are often chewed up by the toothy Baja fish, it is easy and inexpensive to install a new one. Larger leadheads, weighing to six ounces or more, have taken marlin, dorado and albacore when trolled. When dropped to the bottom they are often targeted by grouper, pargo and cabrilla. The best known lures of this type are made by the Scampi Lure Company, San Diego. Other similar types go under the names of Scrounger, Mojo.

Smaller lures are effective around the rocks when trolled, or cast and retreived. Top colors are silver flake, amber flake and green flake. There are many varieties of tails on the market, and all catch fish, but we've found the Scampi brand to be the most durable.

Trolling heads—may range in size from a tiny ten millimeters in diameter to marlin heads which may weigh over a pound. The composition of a completed jig can vary from lead to plastic heads with a wide assortment of trailing plastics, feathers. The line goes through a hole in the head and then to the hook, or hooks. All are designed to "ride up" the line when a fish is hooked to minimize damage to the lure. There are many manufacturers of trolling heads; a few popular West Coast brands include: Seastrike, Patco and Sevenstrand.

Best results with the smaller albacore-type heads come from the colors of white, blue-white, red-white and yellow-green. They may be "stacked" two or three high above the hook, if desired, to present a larger target. When it comes to the large marlin lures, the best colors lie in the yellow-greens, red-white, pink-white and yellow-reds. None of the above means that that old black feathered trolling head lying in the bottom of the jig box won't knock'em dead, because sometimes they do. We're just playing the percentages.

Swimmers—are made of plastic or wood and shaped to simulate a live fish. Variations include sinkers, floaters, divers and poppers. A few even even haves an internal rattle. The swimming lures can draw a lot of attention when trolled — usually slowly — over shallow reefs or through schools of fish. Popular patterns are the mackerel and sardine in blues and greens, and a flourescent hot pink. The latter has proven deadly on cabrilla when nothing else works. Popular brands are Rapala, Rebel and Cordell. Slow trolling, not casting, is usually the best way to use a swimmer. I carry several in my box.

Wahoo Specials—are a group of lures unique unto themselves, thanks to the "hoo's" very special set of dentures and a preference for larger-than-average, fast-moving jigs. The big action on these fish usually comes from trolling, with casting usually serving less effectively. Dark colors predominate on most lures, with a chrome Hopkins spoon a good choice after the school is located.

But before we begin with either mode, get out the heavy wire leader material and put at least a foot in front of anything you are going to toss at them, including live bait. Many anglers also "booby trap" their jigs by adding a hook or two up near the front of the jig. Huge lures 12 to 16 inches long (Braid Products) have been designed just for wahoo. Others wire on trailing hooks six inches or more beyond their normal placement on a jig in the hopes of snagging their prey.

It may seem like a lot of fussing about one fish, but those who catch wahoo will tell you that not only are they razortoothed and incredibly swift, but grilled or smoked, they are some of the best.

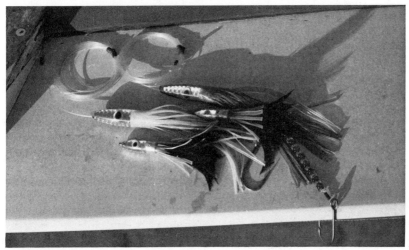

TOM MILLER

These Patco marlin and albacore feathers are only representative of a wide variety of effective trolling heads for Baja.

Though much of this book is directed toward the taking of fish on lures, it would be foolish to ignore bait, for there is much to be said for propelling a tasty tidbit out onto promising waters and waiting to see what develops.

Aside from a few frozen flying fish at the resorts, any baits you might wish to use in Baja are limited to what you can find along the way, or bring with you. If you have a circular throw net, bring it along, there are many opportunities to use one, particularly around Magdalena Bay and in the Sea of Cortez. If you don't have one, it might be worthwhile to buy one and learn to use it. We've have many memorable days using net-caught baitfish, either live or fresh dead, in Baja waters.

We have also found that it is very helpful to watch what the locals are using . . . sometimes the most unusual item will work like a charm. Below are a few notes on what we have found over the years.

Mussels are usually common along the rocks in Zone 1, while sandy beaches often yield Pismo clams and sand crabs. On low tides rocky areas usually provide small crabs, rock clams, a variety of worms and snails, while the esteros may be tapped for ghost shrimp, razor clams, etc. All are excellent baits for onshore action. Salted anchovies from home require little refrigeration but squid should be refrigerated or frozen, while blood worms may last for days in an ice chest.

Clams are also common in Zone II but at times we've resorted to limpets or snails found on the rocks in the intertidal zone. Again watch for small crabs and minnows. Abalone trimmings, when available, make a fine bait.

Around Bahia Magdalena and in the Sea of Cortez one can occasionally purchase shrimp, an exellent bait for any onshore species. Look for clams and crustaceans, such as small crabs, in the esteros or under intertidal rocks.

From Cabo on around into the Cortez, don't hesitate to cut off a portion of fish already caught and cast it into a nearby deep spot. Pargo, members of the jack family, cabrilla and grouper — plus the less desirable triggers and puffers — pick up on these baits, especially at night.

After dark many of the species living just offshore come into the shallows to feed. When looking for the larger species, use a healthy chunk of bait, or a small fish, and cast it onto a sandy spot near some rocks, not into them. This way there is a better chance to set the hook and then fight it in open water.

Outdoor writer and La Paz resident, Jerry Klink, tells of taking a 250 pound grouper night fishing near the rocks by Hotel Punta Colorada. I have seen his efforts also result in pargo, cabrilla, grouper and lesser species. He lists night fishing as a favorite pursuit, because, you never know . . .

One night, while fishing a beach south of La Paz, I took six different species in less than two hours — toro, triggerfish, pargo, cabrilla, chino mero and ladyfish. The evening came to an end when, on my last bait, something grabbed it, and headed for Mazatlan. In less than two minutes I was cleaned out of line.

Flyfishing

It was only a short time ago that you could have put all the fishermen who had tossed a fly into the Sea of Cortez in a small skiff, and still have room for an ice chest full of cerveza. Today the aficianados number in the hundreds, and you will find them regularly in Mulege, Loreto, the East Cape and Cabo, their "long rods" poised to do battle with a wide variey of species.

Nearly 25 years ago Harry Kime, of Orange, California, was one of those who proved that the Cortez was indeed fertile territory for a wide variety of sport species. Harry's stories are many...

He tells of whipping a marlin near Loreto. After carefully gauging his adversary at about 200 pounds, considering that he was alone and carried no gaff, he showed his innate wisdom by releasing it.

The story of flyfishing in Baja waters is not yet complete, but the variety of species taken on the long rod grows each season. I hope that I will have the opportunity to tell it, for it will be an exciting one.

HARRY KIME

These seven yellowtail and one sierra mackerel gave Harry Kime a flyfishing day to remember in Loreto.

One Step From Immortality

It would be a rare person indeed who, having an interest in nature, would not at some time in his lifetime like to be in a position of finding a new species. Whether the find be a bug, beast, fish or plant that defies immediate identification, there is a thrill of discovery. After all, there might be an opportunity to place one's own name, suitably latinized, into the world's taxonomy.

Once, while digging for a dinner of rock clams on an isolated beach near El Rosario, a small creature appeared in the hole I was excavating. Its slimy, two and one-half inch long body was a bright pink and it scooted around the pool in a frenzy. After finally capturing it I discovered that it didn't have any eyes.

The first thing that came to my mind was the pigmetless, blind animals that have evolved in several of the world's underground caverns. After thousands of generations, the lack of need for protective coloration accompanied by a completely dark environment created races of fish, salamanders and crickets which are pink and sightless. On this wild, rocky beach I decided that there must be an entrance to a great undersea cavern.

Queries to several local fishermen resulted only in stares of wonder at my little friend. No one back at Espinoza's Cantina in El Rosario had ever heard of, nor seen, such a fish. Finally I decided to preserve him and return to California for identification. After about 15 minutes of happy imbibing in a jar of vodka, he passed on—happily stoned.

On the way home I speculated on what latinized name I might attach to my charge. Maybe it would be *milleri.* Or should the honor go to Baja California or El Rosario. Maybe the name *espinosiensis* would be worth a free lobster taco and cerveza. Important considerations all.

Two days later I entered the office of John Fitch, the top biologist with the California Department of Fish and Game. He looked up and said, "I see you found a *Typhlogobius californiansis.*" There went the dreams of immortality, the free tacos and cervezas. All my pickled friend had done for me was to ruin about eight ounces of booze. He did, however, lead a rather interesting life.

This Typhlogobius is commonly known as a blind goby and, although rarely seen, is fairly common. They live exclusively in the burrows of the ghost shrimp, *Callianassa affinis.* Here they live in harmony with their hosts who supply them with bits of seaweed and animal matter to eat. They mate for life at the age of six months and the female   may lay as many as 15,000 eggs during its lifetime.

Official measurements of my particular Typhlogobius showed that it was only one-half inch short of a new world record, so in a way, I did become a part of history.

Baja's Fishing Zones

Many times I've sat down at the typewriter to do this section of this book. I find it easy to zero in on a small portion of the Baja peninsula as a particular beach can be described or a fishery delineated; but when it comes to describing all of the conditions and characteristics of more than 2000 miles of shoreline, how they are affected by the oceanic currents, their cool upwellings, the diurnal tidal surges through the narrow portion of the Cortez and the hot winds which blow off the deserts, I am almost at a loss for words.

It is, for this reason, that I have divided the waters around the peninsula into zones, or regions. Each zone is acted upon by a different set of conditions which are not necessarily dictated strictly by its longitude and latitude, but by its currents, tides and temperatures which move in and out of the zone.

ZONE I — Thanks to cold, deep upwellings which come onto the continental shelf south of Ensenada, rockfish are found at depths as shallow as those taken by anglers north of Santa Barbara in California. Yet the warmer surface currents bring northward numbers of heat-loving gamefish such as marlin, dorado, tuna and yellowtail, to name a few.

ZONE II — Further south, past Punta San Eugenio and Cedros Islands, the cooling waters have subsided and the environment offers a refuge for a wealth of yellowtail, tuna, wahoo and bonito. Several species, so abundant in the Cortez, begin to appear here such as the grouper, the cabrilla and the pargo.

ZONE III — This area is unique in that it comprises the largest region of tidal estuaries on the Baja peninsula. Almost untouched by the sport angler, it offers a wide variety of fishing experiences, including world-record size snook, in well protected waters. And just outside are a number of fishing banks which are popular with the San Diego based long-range boats.

ZONE IV — Next comes the Cape of San Lucas, or Cabo, where the cooler Pacific waters are tempered by the warm Cortez to provide an ideal year around environment for a wide variety of highly prized sportfish—marlin (all three varieties), sailfish, dorado, wahoo, tuna and a host of smaller species. Truly a place where fishing fantasies are acted out amid luxury hotels, sleek yachts and feeding fish.

ZONE V — That first portion which lies entirely within the Sea of Cortez is given the name of East Cape, for it is only a few miles away and offers much the same fishing. Here life is simpler and the conversation at the modest fishing lodges is almost always centered on tight lines and big fish. Many world records have been taken in this area.

ZONE VI — La Paz is where it all began. Forty years ago a trickle of adventurers armed with fishing rods began to appear in the dusty streets of La Paz. They bartered with the natives for rides in leaky dugout canoes and hit the jackpot. The stories spread and the stream of Baja bound anglers grows wider and stronger each year.

ZONE VII — Private airplanes supplemented by several small airlines have transformed the resource-rich, but sparsely settled, Zone VII into one of the world's finest small gamefish destinations. Until the paved highway opened in 1973, nearly all visitors came by air to savor the primitive charm and excellent fishing. With the highway, the tourist has become a way of life with the natives whose numbers have swelled with migrants from mainland Mexico in search of work in an active economy.

ZONE VIII — To many the Midriff Zone brings an excitement which is addictive. Each spring and summer the many islands are literally surrounded by teeming hordes of sealife. For six months, or more, an eat-and-be-eaten orgy occurs almost everywhere, and thousands of anglers come to take their share. Despite little water and few facilities, the Midriff continues to draw large numbers of Baja visitors.

ZONE IX — Almost a sea to itself, this zone is the most visited of all thanks to its close proximity to the border. Miles of unspoiled sandy beaches attract many weekend visitors, plus numbers of "snowbirds" who trailer south to escape the snowy rigors of their home states. Local fishing, once bountiful, is generally restricted to the corvina family, but usually suffices for as many excellent dinners as one might wish.

ZONE X — Why, do you say, does Zone X even exist when it is shown on the map only as an arrow pointing off the page? Well, it is visited by nearly 1000 record-seeking fishermen each year who board the sleek and modern long-range fishing boats in San Diego. After a voyage of nearly 1000 miles, a small chain of islands appears whose surrounding reefs are populated with what are probably the largest concentration of record breaking yellowfin tuna anywhere in the world. These, along with the large numbers of wahoo, serve to attract anglers from all over the world.

Now, with that let's look closer at each Baja Fishing Zone.

TYPES OF FISHING

Types of fishing shown on Baja Angling Maps are:

Onshore (from shore, intertidal) ✳✳ ✳✳ ✳ ✳✳✳

Inshore (to about 100 fathoms)

Rockcod (Pacific side)

Offshore (deepwater trolling)

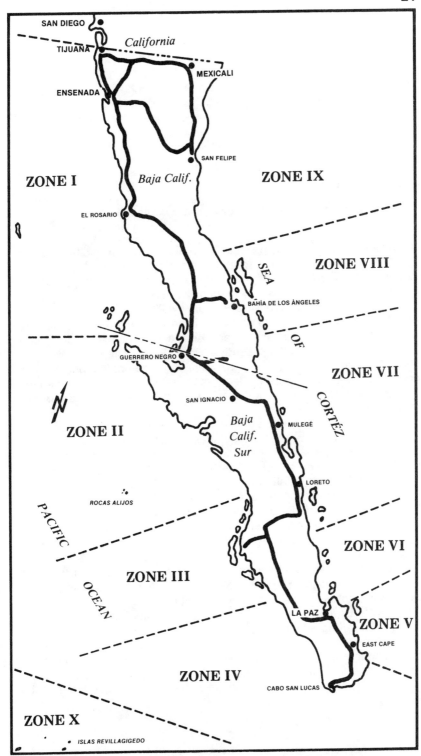

Zone I:　North Pacific Coast

The general character of Baja California's northern Pacific coast is that of the state of California south of Point Conception, but without the sprawling megalopolis which extends from Santa Barbara to San Diego. Except for the series of small settlements culminating in the city of Ensenada, it is rare that you will see much evidence of human habitation.

The more than 500 miles of coastline between the border and Punta San Eugenio offer a mix of sandy beaches and rocky points, crashing surf and calm esteros. Upwellings south of Punta Banda bring cool waters to coastal shores, providing an environment for huge populations of rock-cod in waters as shallow as 120 feet. As the effect subsides to the south, the water warms again, and will average about five degrees warmer than that found off Southern California.

Outside, along the 100 fathom line, warm currents act as a pathway for a variety of migrating fish. Schools of albacore come north from beyond Guadalupe Island; marlin, yellowfin tuna, skipjack and dorado ride the warming waters past Cedros Island to as far north as the Channel Islands off Southern California. Migrations of more inshore types— yellowtail, barracuda, bonito and white seabass—follow the schools of forage fish as they move along the coastal reefs. The range of most on-shore species found in Southern California extends as far south as Punta Eugenio. One notable exception is the barred surfperch which disappears near El Rosario.

As you proceed south from the border there is less rain from the winter storms sweeping from the North Pacific and the leafy vegetation reflects it. Cactus is more and more evident until it predominates around Scammon's Lagoon where the average annual rainfall is less than three inches. Prevailing winds become somewhat stronger and often raise large whitecaps around Cedros. Fog and low clouds may be expected during spring and summer months but they usually clear by noon... about the same time the breezes start. Generally, temperatures are comfortable, averaging only a few degrees higher than those experienced in San Diego.

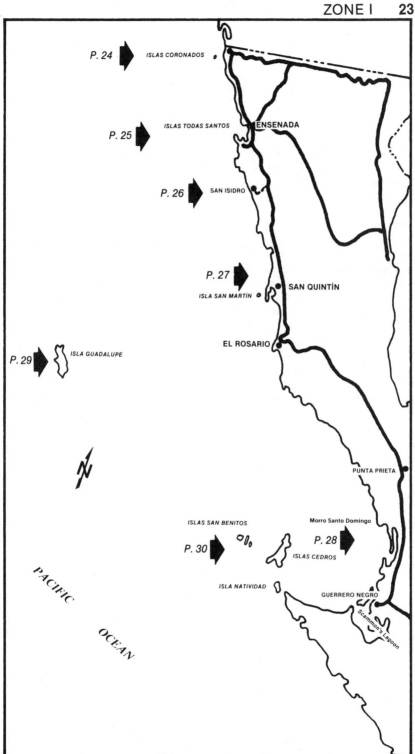

P. 24 ▶ ISLAS CORONADOS

P. 25 ▶ ISLAS TODAS SANTOS   ENSENADA

P. 26 ▶ SAN ISIDRO

P. 27 ▶ SAN QUINTÍN
ISLA SAN MARTÍN

EL ROSARIO

P. 29 ▶ ISLA GUADALUPE

PUNTA PRIETA

ISLAS SAN BENITOS   Morro Santo Domingo

P. 30 ▶   P. 28 ▶
ISLAS CEDROS

ISLA NATIVIDAD   GUERRERO NEGRO
Scammon's Lagoon

PACIFIC OCEAN

Los Coronados

Located only 13 nautical miles south of San Diego's Point Loma, the Coronado Islands are more heavily fished than any other part of Mexico. From April through September, dozens, and sometimes hundreds, of boats course the predawn darkness to get into position for the anticipated early bite of yellowtail.

This is one of the few areas in Mexico that has been closed to commercial netting and reserved for sportfishing. The resource holds up well considering the heavy pressure applied by the San Diego based boats. Bonito, barracuda, white seabass and rockfish are also taken there.

Probably 90 percent of the albacore taken by Southern Californians are found to the west and south of the islands. Boats range as much as 100 miles into Mexican waters to search out the albacore in such places as the Dumping Grounds, Sixty Mile Bank, 213 Fathom Spot and other undersea mountaintops which dot the outer continental shelf as far as Guadalupe Island. Usually beginning in late June and extending through September, fully 150,000 tickets will be sold to anglers wishing to load up on the "chicken of the sea" in the waters of Mexico.

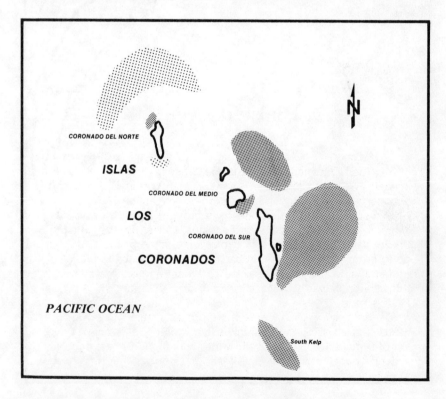

CORONADO DEL NORTE

ISLAS

CORONADO DEL MEDIO

LOS

CORONADO DEL SUR

CORONADOS

PACIFIC OCEAN

South Kelp

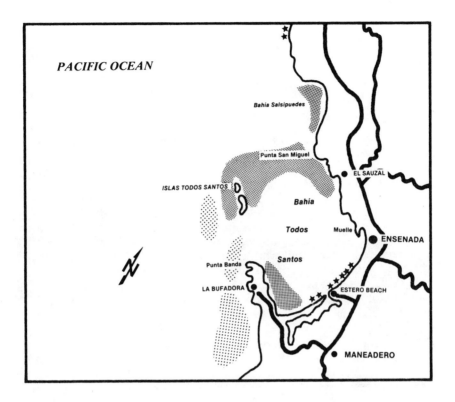

PACIFIC OCEAN

Bahia Salsipuedes

Punta San Miguel

EL SAUZAL

ISLAS TODOS SANTOS

Bahía

Todos   Muelle   ENSENADA

Santos

Punta Banda

LA BUFADORA

ESTERO BEACH

MANEADERO

A Place To Watch

As late as 1965 from May through Thanksgiving, the first port south of the border, Ensenada, was a prime prospect for a lot of action on yellowtail and white seabass. But as in many areas of the world, the pressures of an exploding population—such as over exploitation of natural resources and pollution—have brought about a drastic drop in the angler success for these two species. Currently, the city and port authority have joined in an effort to reverse some of the problems and hope to bring Ensenada fishing back to the excellence for which it was once famous. In the meantime, the partyboat anglers are still enjoying better fishing for barracuda and bonita than is found north of the border in California.

Just south of Punta Banda there are a number of very productive rockcod spots. Due to the cool upwelling which occurs below the point, much of the action takes place in water less than 200 feet deep.

Keep your eye on Ensenada for it just could come back as Baja's best easy-to-reach fishery.

A Highly Visitable Spot

One area along Baja's Pacific side that I never get tired of visiting is San Isidro and Castro's Camp. Located 12 miles off the paved road and 60 miles south of Ensenada, the area exhibits the atmosphere of a typical Mexican fishing village. At the small cove of San Ysidro, the Castro family has established a small fishing operation. And what fishing! Many times I've returned from Castro's with an ice chest full of fillets.

Drawn by the cool ocean upwelling which occurs south of Ensenada, the nearby reefs are loaded with many varieties of rockcod, whitefish and large ling cod. In season, white seabass, yellowtail, black sea bass, barracuda and bonito also make their presence known. Fishing from large skiffs, the best action is usually obtained with yo-yo type jigs over the 150 foot deep reefs, although some prefer to bait rockcod ganions with pieces of squid.

Onshore anglers will find a wide variety of surf fishing conditions within a ten mile radius of Castro's. A sandy beach five miles north at Punta Cabras has proven particularly productive for barred perch.

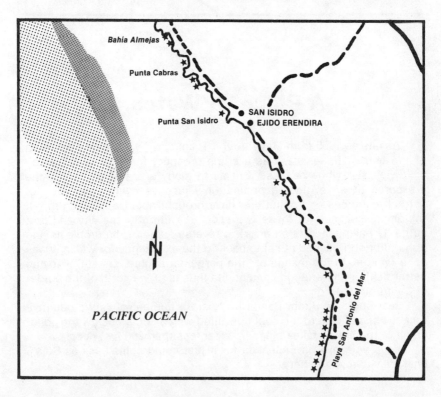

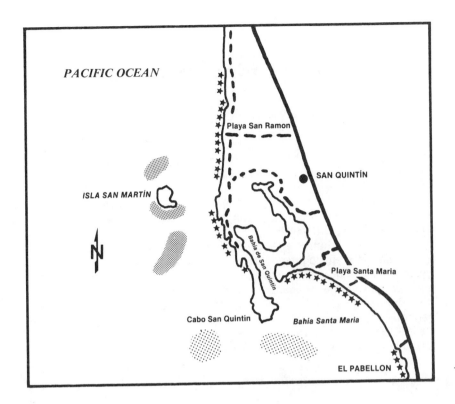

Perch — Big and Plenty

Nowhere in its range are the barred perch any bigger, or more plentiful, than along the beaches which extend about 20 miles in both directions from the commulity of San Quintin. From the clam beds of Playa San Ramon to Rancho Soccoro's pebbly beaches, they may be taken in great numbers at almost any time of the year on Pismo clams and fresh-dead anchovies.

Once a neighbor, Al Teachout, and I went to a cobblestoned beach just to the south of Punta Colonet and found the perch literally boiling in the shallow surf. By casting only 30 feet, we were hooking two-pounders like mad. Within 30 minutes we had taken our self-imposed limits of ten each and started releasing what we took. A young boy appeared behind us and we offered to give him as many as he wanted to take home for his family. He said he had eight brothers and sisters, so we filled a sack with 30 fish and took him home as he couldn't carry it alone. His grateful mother picked us several dozen relleno-type chiles and a huge cauliflower to take along. Another profitable day of fishing.

Other fish which are plentiful in the area are spotfin and yellowfin croaker and huge jacksmelt.

Surf Fishing Paradise

In late November a few years ago, Jack Ridenoure and I found ourselves about to give up waiting out a cold, rainy wind at Bahia de Los Angeles. In three days we hadn't been near the water. As a last hope of salvaging something from our trip, we checked the map for a sheltered spot on the Pacific side of the peninsula.

We decided to try for a tiny dot on the map in the lee of a point named Santo Domingo. Located about an hour's drive south of Parador Punta Prieta, it turned out to be just what we wanted—warm, dry, calm and had lots of surf fish.

Almost immediately after breaking out the light (four to six pound) tackle we were struggling with spotfin croaker. Some of our catch weighed as much as six pounds, and we will always wonder about the ones which were never headed.

Another time, in June, the water was full of corbina. By standing perfectly still, three and four pounders came to feed within three feet of my toes. The only bait we had, mussels, got us all of the fish we wanted. I have never been skunked at Puerto Santo Domingo.

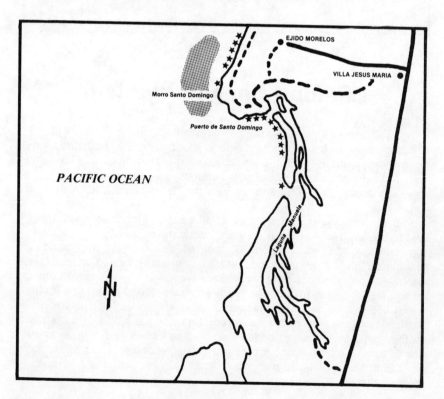

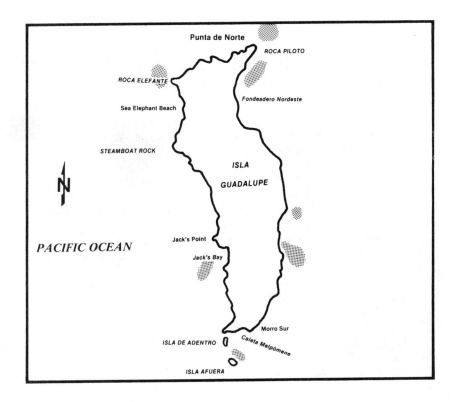

The First Long-Range Trip

In the 1930s, the late Frank Kessig, owner of one of San Diego's sportfishing landings, took some of his friends and customers out to Guadalupe Island, 220 miles to the southwest. From stories of large herds of yellowtail and great bluefin tuna told by returning commercial fishermen, he felt that it warranted taking a small, slow boat that far. And what a trip it was!

In less than two days the men put several hundred yellows and one bluefin tuna on the deck. Story has it that the tuna weighed "only" 60 pounds and the yellows averaged over 30 pounds; but they lost others because they couldn't stop them. The fish literally destroyed everyone's tackle.

In 1939, when I was 11, my Dad and I went to meet Captain Kessig's returning boat and he told me I could have any fish that I could lift off the boat. I couldn't get even the smallest over the rail and onto the dock!

Guadalupe is still visited by the long-range boats, especially during the winter on four and five day trips; and recent years have shown that there are still many fish to be taken which top the 40 pound mark.

A World To Itself

The cluster of offshore islands northwest of Punta Eugenio offers a variety of interests to the visitor. From Cedros millions of tons of salt, from the world's largest evaporative salt works at Guerrero Negro, are loaded into large cargo liners for shipment to chemical plants worldwide. A cannery also processes fish for international markets.

A small fishing camp on the easternmost side of the three San Benito Islands is a favorite stopping place for the long-range boats where they barter for a supply of lobster and abalone to feed their passengers. Once, while anchored there, several of us began chumming a few live baits and throwing jigs. Within minutes we were taking barracuda, kelp bass and small yellowtail with almost every cast. Later, while on a nearby night anchorage, we caught about 40 yellows from 35 to 45 pounds using slabs from the barracuda and small yellows. The action lasted all night.

The best kelp bass fishing I have ever experienced was at San Benito; nearly every fish exceeded five pounds and were taken on a light spinning rig and 12-pound test line.

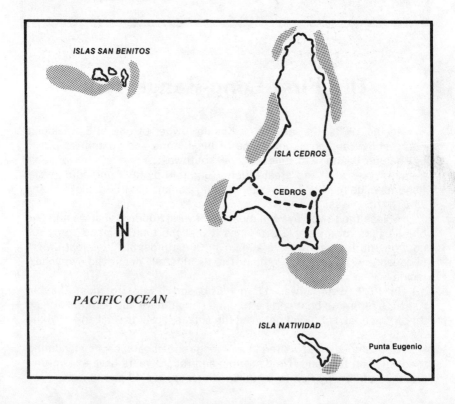

BILL BEEBE

The sandy beaches and rocky shores of Baja's northern Pacific coast yield a wide variety of species for the shore angler.

CARL BITTNER

The 1928 Chevrolet in the background dates this picture of Herman Handshy and Carl Bittner with yellowtail at Punta Banda.

Zone II: Central Pacific Coast

There is no greater wealth of fish and other sealife along Baja's Pacific than in its Central section. Surely, if the sometimes-graded access roads were paved and if fresh water were more plentiful, this region would undoubtedly see many thousands of norteamericano visitors.

A surf fisherman would have more than 280 miles of sandy beaches interspersed with rocky points, plus a number of large tidal lagoons, on which to plant his sandspike. And he wouldn't likely be bored, for the skilled angler would be able to locate good populations of members of the croaker family such as corvina, spotfin croaker and yellowfin croaker. Around the rocky points lie numerous rockdwellers which are susceptible to a piece of clam or crustacean.

Presently the many inshore reefs are fished only by the Mexican fisherman and the long-range sportfishers out of San Diego. But with paving you would see many small boats joining in the pursuit of the large populations of yellowtail, grouper, white seabass and other species which readily take jigs and bait.

Punta Abreojos is considered the northern limit of many of the more tropical species found to the south and in the Cortez.

The lagoons, or esteros, of Pond, Coyote and San Ignacio offer a mixture of small species, plus clams and oysters, to the visitor. Mangrove trees make their appearance around Abreojos and bring the possibility of snook into view. Highly sought in the subtropical Atlantic, the snook's extend here is still relatively unknown.

At these latitudes the influence of the tropics becomes more apparent. Though the typical spring-summer low clouds continue, they are less prevalent and burn off readily in the hot sun. Rain clouds usually appear during the August-October "chubasco" season when tropical storms sometimes get this far north. Local winter fogs show at times, influenced by the warm currents offshore.

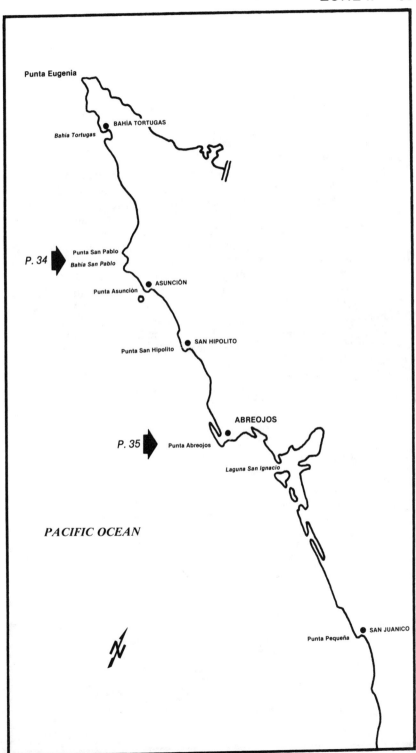

The Honey Pot

When the San Diego boats leave on their six to eight day Baja fishing trips you can be sure that their plans call for a stop around Bahia San Pablo. This region is looked upon by many of the skippers as a "sure action" spot when all others fail. There are numerous pinnacles and reefs between Punta San Pablo and Isla Asuncion that attract good numbers of yellowtail the year around. Though the average size probably does not exceed ten pounds, the action is often nonstop.

Once, during a November trip, we had scratched only a few fish each from such spots as Benitos, Alijos Rocks and the Uncle Sam Banks so we headed for San Pablo. The first strike came about daylight and continued nonstop for almost eight hours; the last three of those saw us taking nearly 100 nice dorado from the thousands which joined the chum line. No records were set, but, again, San Pablo saved the trip.

If you are equipped to drive to these shores from the distant Mexico 1, you will be treated to some very fine surf fishing and many clamming areas.

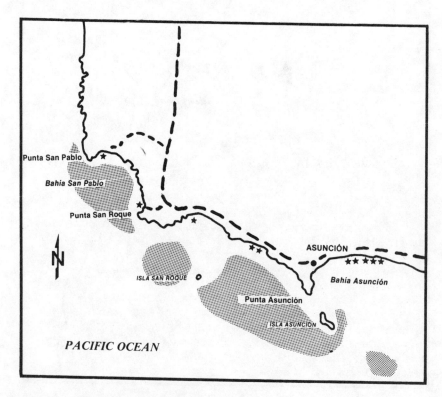

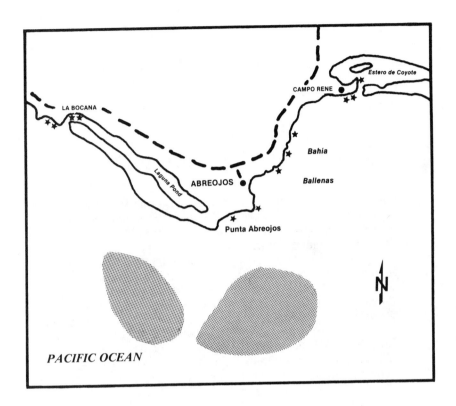

Abreojos — An Eye Opener

You almost need a 4X4 for this one—or a plane. Located 60 miles off the paved Mexico 1, the Abreojos area has an almost seasonless supply of fish suitable for the onshore and inshore angler. It abounds with lobster, abalone and clams to round out the camper's seafood diet. Services are limited to fuel, a few groceries, a "loncheria" or two and some rustic cabins at Campo Rene.

The beaches, rocky points and mouths of the esteros all have a wide variety of fish for the light tackle shorecaster. These include croaker, corvina, corbina, halibut and triggerfish. With a boat the nearby reefs may be fished for yellowtail, black sea bass and white seabass—even dorado in the late summer.

But it is the mangrove-lined channels of Estero Coyote which hold the most interest for me. Trolling and casting jigs or Rapala lures have brought numerous strikes and memorable battles with grouper, cabrilla and a number of unknowns which we never got to the boat. The area is a challenge because the line-catching tangle of mangrove roots lie only a few feet away.

Zone III   Magdalena Bay

Though Magdalena Bay has been fished commercially for some years, only recently has it received attention from American anglers. Actually a series of bays and inlets which are interconnected by more than 120 miles of inland waterways, it is protected from the Pacific by dark volcanic peaks and long white sand dunes. Inland lies the low and dry Madgalena Plain. Years could be spent exploring this region.

Navigable over its entire length with a shallow-draft boat, it offers almost unlimited opportunities for angling adventure. Many species are in the baylets, mangrove-lined channels and around the Pacific Ocean entrances. Snook, croaker, corvina, yellowtail, small grouper, cabrilla, pargo, and sierra are only a portion of the list of fish to be found In the area.

The only villages where limited supplies are available are Puerto San Carlos and Puerto Astorga (Puerto Lopez Mateos on some maps). The balance has a scattering of small and usually seasonal fish camps reached by often-sandy, unimproved roads.

Outside there are numerous reefs which often provide "super" fishing. The Thetis and Uncle Sam Banks are among those visited regularly by the San Diego based long-range boats where they take yellowtail, dorado, wahoo, yellowfin tuna and black sea bass. Some smaller inner reefs are accessible to larger trailered boats which may be launched at San Carlos.

Shore angling on both the surf and bay sides of the islands is excellent with halibut, corvina and croaker making up most of the catch. Additionally the area provides a winter home to literally millions of migratory birds.

This zone's climate is tempered by the large surface area of warm waters. Local fogs and low mists are common at night and during early morning hours during winter and spring. Most winds are also local, although occasional high winds accompanied by rain occur during the August-October "chubasco" season. Residents claim that Magdalena has the most temperate climate in all of Baja.

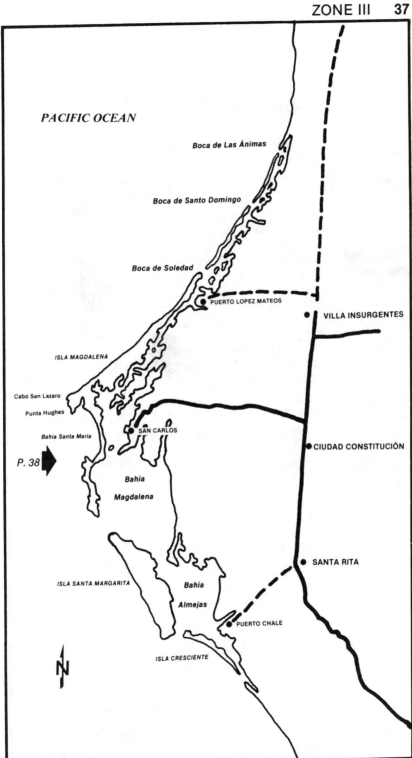

PACIFIC OCEAN

Boca de Las Ánimas

Boca de Santo Domingo

Boca de Soledad

PUERTO LOPEZ MATEOS

VILLA INSURGENTES

ISLA MAGDALENA

Cabo San Lazaro

Punta Hughes

Bahia Santa Maria

P. 38

SAN CARLOS

CIUDAD CONSTITUCIÓN

Bahía

Magdalena

SANTA RITA

ISLA SANTA MARGARITA

Bahía

Almejas

PUERTO CHALE

ISLA CRESCIENTE

N

Snook Country?

Since the norteamericano first began driving south to fish the waters of Baja there have been stories of huge black snook, or robalo, living in the brackish lagoons along the southern half of the peninsula. The late Ray Cannon told of having seen a harpooned snook taken from the river at Mulege that approximated 80 pounds, nearly twice the existing world record. I saw a 41 pounder weighed in on IGFA-approved scales that was taken near Hotel Punta Colorada in an area where there is supposed to be an underwater spring.

But it is in the Magdalena Bay complex where the largest population of record breakers is likely to exist. The mangroves contain hundreds of miles of ideal habitat. The manager of the local fisherman's cooperative told me that several snook weighing over 60 pounds are brought in each year by the commercial fishermen. I saw one that approximated 40 pounds live weight. Several times I've seen huge splashes or watched large shadows glide through the mangrove roots, but I've never caught even a small one. Others have, but I guess I haven't developed that skill yet. Maybe one of these days.

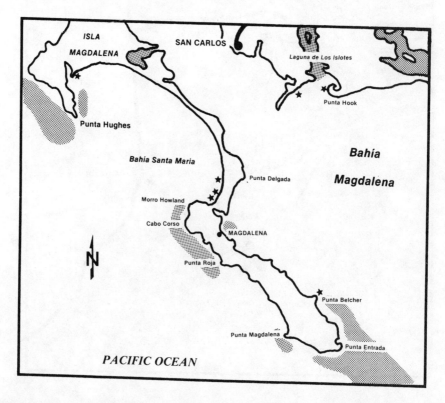

This 41 pound, 8 ounce black snook gave Sam Sanet of Florida a fish to remember.

Zone IV: Cabo—The Cape

At the point where the long rocky finger of land known as Baja California collapses into the sea, the Pacific Ocean shifts a portion of its richness into a 700 mile-long cleft in the earth's crust to form an even richer body of water, the Sea of Cortez. And it is in the Cabo Zone where numerous migrating gamefish join resident species before following their traditional paths through the Cortez and the Eastern Pacific.

The less than 100 miles of shoreline consists of innumerable rocky promontories and small sandy beaches where the onshore angler, working the dawn and dusk, can cast jigs to all sorts of gamefish. Yellowtail, roosterfish, toro, sierra, cabrilla, grouper, pompano and pargo are only a portion of the list. Though the size of these fish rarely exceeds 15 pounds, they can provide a thrilling time.

Cabo is THE destination for anyone looking for a billfish or dorado any time of the year. Though the supply varies with the months—November-May being the best—they are there all of the time. Winter and early spring is an ideal time for those with their own small boats because winds then are rarely a problem.

There are a number of productive reefs located in this zone: the Jamie and Golden Gate Banks are found on the Pacific side; the inner and outer sections of the Gordo Banks are 20 miles east of the Cape and boast good populations of wahoo during the winter and spring. Additionally, there are a number of rocky shelves which extend out from shore, the best of which is off Cabo Falso.

Facilities exist around San Lucas for launching, repairs (though parts are scarce, the mechanics are good), fuel and food. Fishing tackle is hard to find almost everywhere in Mexico.

There are numerous accommodations in the area but it is wise to make reservations well ahead of time and also arrange for boat rentals during the crowded November-June season.

This area's weather is the envy of the world; warm, almost windless days predominate during the winter and spring. Summer and fall have onshore breezes to temper the hot sun and swells come from the southern quadrant, caused by tropical storms spawned in the warm seas west of Acapulco. These disturbances sometimes strike the peninsula and their fringes provide most of the 10-12 inches of rain received annually.

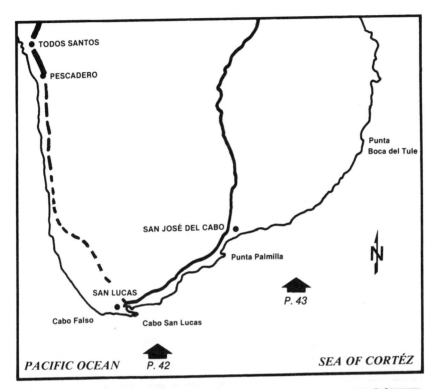

TODOS SANTOS

PESCADERO

Punta
Boca del Tule

SAN JOSÉ DEL CABO

Punta Palmilla

N

P. 43

SAN LUCAS

Cabo Falso   Cabo San Lucas

PACIFIC OCEAN   P. 42   *SEA OF CORTÉZ*

*Cabo's billfishing variety is shown in these blue, striped and black marlin.
Weights; 580, 150 and 250 pounds, respectively.*

Those Glamour Fish

Whether it be in January, June, August or November, chances are that a week's fishing around Cabo San Lucas will get you at least one of fishdom's glamour fish: marlin (striped, blue or black), sailfish, dorado, wahoo, yellowfin tuna or roosterfish. The marriage of the rich waters of the Cortez and the Pacific at "Land's End" has proven ideal for these and many more species.

Four years ago, John Belmonte, of Los Angeles, bought a 23-foot Skipjack boat and began trailering his rig back and forth about four times a year. His log, to date, shows more than 100 striped marlin, two blue marlin (plus more than 30 lost), a black, 27 sailfish, 40 dorado (over 30 pounds), several dozen roosterfish (one of 71 pounds) with uncounted wahoo and yellowfin tuna. His whole Baja angling experience began a month before he bought the boat when he flew to Cabo for a week's fishing...a true case of fishing pox.

A strong conservationist, Belmonte tags and releases his billfish and brings to the dock only those edibles which he knows will be used. He, and others like him, tag and release thousands of fish each year along the coast of Baja.

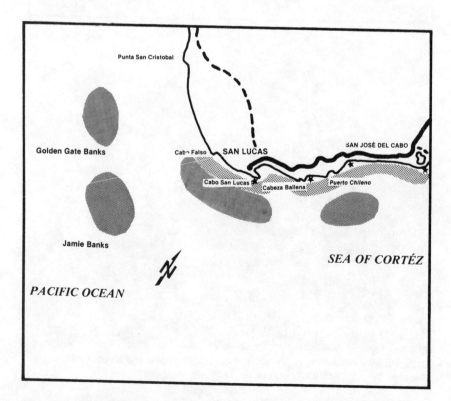

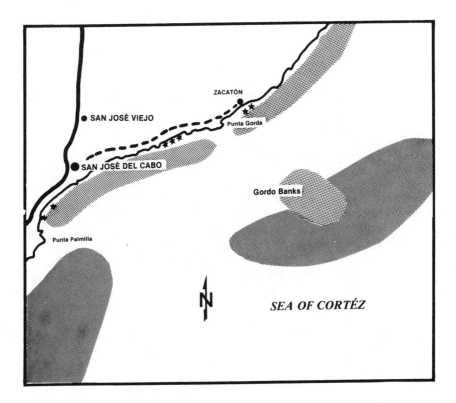

The Wahoo Banks

On the navigation maps of the area the two seamounts, which rise to as close as eight fathoms below the surface, are identified as the Inner and Outer Gorda Banks. In my fishing log they are called the Wahoo Banks. And they truly are for some who have fished these spots. Yet to others, years of fishing there have netted them only an occasional encounter with these speedy members of the mackerel family. The difference is the time of day.

Those who are bent on taking wahoo make it a point to be fishing as the dawn begins breaking in the east, for it is those first two hours of the morning which will provide ten times the wahoo action one is likely to find later in the day. Since this fact was discovered a few years ago, hundreds have had the times of their lives battling these fish.

To try to fish for wahoo at the Gordo Banks from a chartered hotel cruiser is almost a waste of time, for they rarely leave their moorings before seven o'clock. Your best bet is to have your own boat or charter a native "ponga" from the fish camp located a couple of miles east of the town of San Jose del Cabo.

Zone V: The East Cape

This zone provides an ideal combination of nearshore subterranean canyons, reefs and sandy bottoms in a warm, food-rich environment to keep all manner of sportfish in the area the entire year. The zone is entirely within the tranquil confines of the Sea of Cortez and thus experiences little of the heavy swells and crashing waves characteristic of the Pacific side of the peninsula.

The only readily accessible portion of the 65 miles of the East Cape is near the center where the transpeninsular highway comes out of the arroyo from La Paz and touches the Cortez briefly before returning inland on the way to Cabo San Lucas. The balance is best attempted in pickups or off-road vehicles.

Much of the coast in this zone is made up of long sweeping sandy beaches with boulders located just offshore. Only a few rocky headlands break this pattern. In two places the 100 fathom line comes to within a few hundred yards of the shore—at Los Frailes and four miles north of Los Barriles. Here yellowfin tuna are found literally within casting distance of the shore angler. Casting small lures from the beach at dawn usually brings good action for a variety of small gamesters. A chunk of bait tossed out onto the sand and boulder bottoms at night is a good way to connect with a pargo.

Boat anglers in the East Cape can select a wide variety of bottom structures over which they may seek action. From April through December—and occasionally all year—striped marlin and dorado dominate the action along the 100 fathom line. Inside, during the May-November period, the roosterfish provide exciting action within yards of the sandy beaches. Resident species, such as cabrilla, grouper, pargo and amberjack, plus visiting wahoo, pompano and yellowtail, are only a portion of the potential takers of a lure.

All of the half-dozen resorts in the East Cape are well equipped to handle the serious angler—experienced captains with well maintained boats and rental tackle are a trademark of the area. Launching of a trailered boat is usually done over sand beaches. Cartoppers, usually aluminum 15-footers with a high freeboard, are popular and provide greater mobility.

Weather here is moderate year around, with humidity causing occasional discomfort during August and September when most of the area's precipitation occurs. Prevailing winds are from the north during November through March and from the south the balance of the year. Strongest winds occur during January and February.

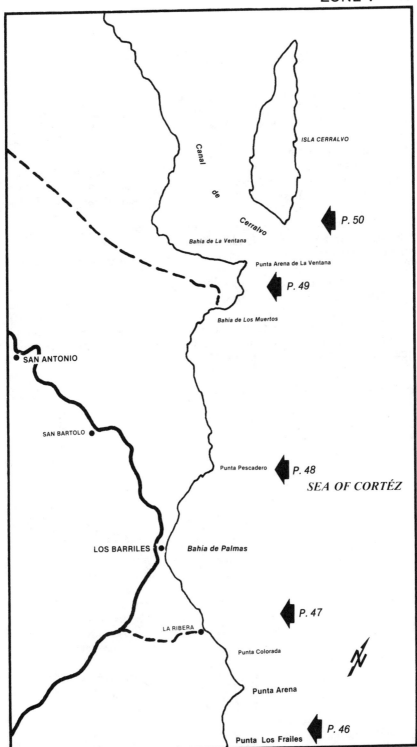

Frustration At Frailes

The small bay on the south side of tall and rocky Punta Los Frailes is unique. The deep cleft in the ocean bottom comes to within yards of a sandy beach with sounding of up to 100 fathoms within casting distance of shore. Caves in the steep canyon walls hold numbers of large black sea bass and grouper; huge roosterfish climb from the depths to chase the schools of mullet; and yellowfin tuna and sailfish have been observed breezing the surface. Divers tell of seeing the silvery forms of tuna "too big to even consider spearing" rising from the dark abyss to snap up a mackerel.

I once spent the better part of an afternoon casting every type of jig I possessed into a school of feeding tuna but with no success—we could see them smashing the bait with their jaws—and I was standing in knee-deep water!

A friend tells of watching a sailfish take a mullet and streaking for the open sea, completely burning out his companion's reel in the process.

Los Frailes and the beaches in both directions are very rewarding to the small boater and shore angler, but beware of the long and often poor road into the area from the paved Mexico 1.

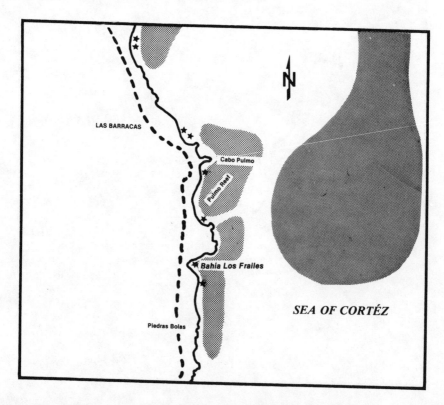

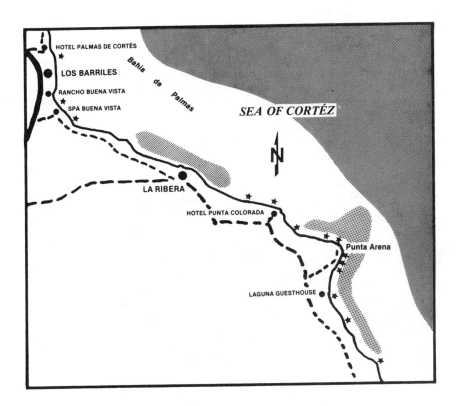

Pez Gallo

From May through October in the area of Punta Arena, the roosters —pez gallo—hold court over the shallow sand and rocky bottoms. The water is often clear enough to see them stalk the bait, then in a splashing rush gobble it and head for cover. Once hooked, the rooster may jump and head to sea or dive under the boat. . . but let me tell you of one pez gallo.

I was using a light (15 pound test) spinning outfit one very calm morning when a big rooster took my mullet. He had missed it a couple of times before he made contact and that made him a bit irritated. He cleared the water twice, then, like a runaway locomotive, headed directly for shore. The next thing I knew he was a good six feet up on the sand. After lying there for a minute, he flopped back into the water and came under the boat. While I scrambled to the other side, he reversed and went back under the boat. This time he stopped in the surfline, turned, jumped and went down the beach with us in mad pursuit. After 45 minutes he gave up. We clipped the line and released a worthy adversary weighing about 30 pounds.

Fisherman's Point

It translates to "fisherman's point," and Punta Pescadero is just that. From the veranda of the beautiful hotel located there, I've watched anglers in the hotel's boats battle large fish within shouting distance of me. One, a dog snapper of over 75 pounds, kept a man from Omaha sweating for over an hour on 60 pound tackle before he subdued it. He waved, I tipped my cerveza in salute and readied myself to hear his story later in the day.

To the north of the point, numerous shallow inshore reefs yield lots of action, especially to the twilight or dawn shore angler. The camper can follow the road north for another five miles, passing many excellent fishing beaches. Several times, in June, I've seen roosterfish working mullet within a dozen feet of shore in this area.

About four miles below is the famous Tuna Hole. Yellowfin tuna lurk almost all year in the deep channel which comes to within a few yards of shore. During the summer months this stretch of boulder-strewn beach is also populated with roosterfish. The onshore angler will find many hookups in here but few will be taken because of the rocks.

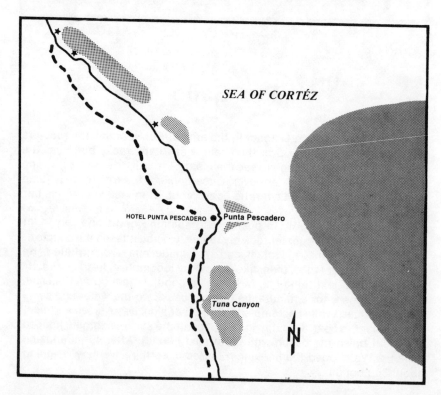

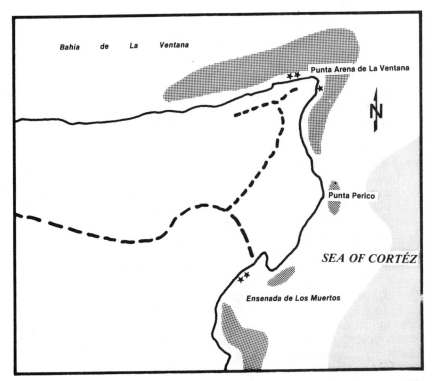

Punta Arena De La Ventana

This sandy point is one of the real comers in Baja fishing. Previously it was little visited, except by a few campers with cartop boats and seasonal commercial fishermen. Quickly the word is getting out that here may well be the best variety of gamefish available anywhere in Baja. As the new Hotel Las Arenas is within yards of the place the word should spread rapidly. Here the concept of fishing from small boats, such as the native 22-foot pangas really comes into its own. There is little to offer in the way of safe anchorages here, thus the need for smaller beachable boats is important.

Extensive boulder-strewn and sandy shallows form ideal habitat for large numbers of roosterfish, plus plenty of pargo and cabrilla. From the shore there are numerous opportunities to take a dozen species of shallow-water dwellers with a variety of light lures. The channel between here and Isla Cerralvo is a well used pathway for migrating fish, and it is not unusual for dorado to appear close to shore in Bahia de Los Muertos, just to the south.

As we learn the area the stories become more numerous, including acrobatic sabalo and speedy toro ripping up light tackle; roosters taking bait within 100 feet of shore in front of the hotel; huge pargo colorado stockpiling my terminal tackle in the rocks, cabrilla to 8 pounds pounding Scampi tails from the rocks in front of the hotel. La Ventana, a place that offers my kind of fishing.

The Remote Cerralvo

One of the least fished portions of the Lower Cortez is the south end of Isla Cerralvo. Located too far from the East Cape resorts or La Paz to be visited regularly, it receives most of its attention from the nearby Hotel Las Arenas and a group of commercial fishermen at adjacent Punta Arena de La Ventana.

From April through November the action over the reef and adjacent dropoff below Punta Sudeste can be almost beyond belief. The times that I've been in the area we've taken or seen, marlin, sailfish, wahoo, dorado, amberjack, yellowfin tuna, cabrilla, pargo and grouper over this and nearby reefs. In late May of 1976 several of us cast sardine-colored Straggler (now Seastrike) jigs into a huge concentration of working fish and hooked barrilete, wahoo or amberjack on every cast. One of our group even had a marlin take his jig and then toss it after a couple of jumps. The mele continued for at least an hour before subsiding.

On another trip I took three nice pargo off Punta Viejos and then had my reel stripped by some unknown protagonist.

Late in the summer of 1983 two of us, fishing from a Hotel Las Arenas panga, made one stop on a school of yellowfin tuna near Roca Montana and an hour later we had a boat full of tuna without ever restarting the motor. Plan a visit to this region.

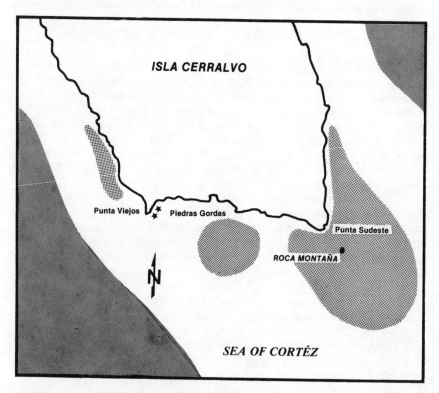

This roosterfish gained the full respect of former Dallas Cowboy quarter-back, Don Meredith.

Zone VI: La Paz

It was in La Paz that the legends of Baja fishing began during the 1930's when a trickle of Americans began appearing in what was then a very sleepy little town. Armed with bamboo and hickory trolling rods and fishing from leaky homemade boats they ventured a short distance outside the harbor entrance in search of fish. And find them they did; marlin, sailfish and dorado appeared in storied numbers. It was not unusual to hook a dozen billfish a day.

Today modern cruisers range beyond Espiritu Santo Island to take marlin, sails, yellowfin tuna and dorado from the diminishing stocks of these gamesters. Still there is plenty of action, despite their lesser numbers. Closer, in the large Bahia de La Paz and along the western escarpments of Espiritu Santo and adjoining Partida Island, the boats find yellowtail, cabrilla, pargo, roosterfish, pompano and sierra.

On extended multi-day trips out of La Paz, the islands of San Francisco and San Jose, plus the nearby Baja coast, offer virtually untouched reefs and shoals to the angler looking for the ultimate in small game fishing. For the diver, there are worlds of underwater wonders.

Lack of access to much of the shoreline in the La Paz Zone somewhat restricts the surf fisherman to a few miles of beach west and north of La Paz, or a few difficult-to-reach spots such as Punta Coyote and Bahia Rosario to the east. These spots are rather heavily fished by commercial fishermen so the pickings can be lean, except for flurries supplied by migrating schools of sierra, toro and yellowtail, plus a few cabrilla and pargo.

Rocky cliffs dominate much of this zone's coastal portions. The long sandy stretch of the Mogote, which forms the La Paz Harbor, is the main smooth beach. Aside from a few others on the islands and along the east side, the balance of the beaches are covered with pebbles and small rocks. On the nearby islands there are many well protected coves which offer secluded campsites for the boater.

Once away from the prevailing coastal breezes, the region can be very hot anytime from April through October, but when on the water it is usually more comfortable and rarely unbearable. Most of the rains come during the August-October "chubasco" season. Hurricanes occur maybe once every five years. Winter prevailing winds are from the north; summer are from the southeast.

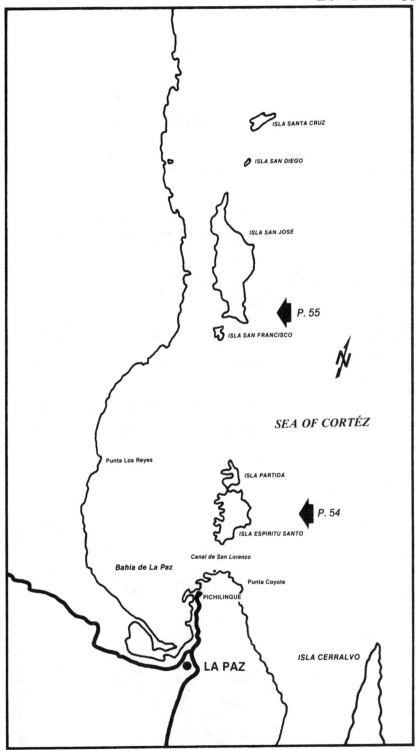

ISLA SANTA CRUZ

ISLA SAN DIEGO

ISLA SAN JOSÉ

P. 55

ISLA SAN FRANCISCO

N

SEA OF CORTÉZ

Punta Los Reyes

ISLA PARTIDA

P. 54

ISLA ESPÍRITU SANTO

Canal de San Lorenzo

Bahía de La Paz

Punta Coyote

PICHILINGUE

LA PAZ

ISLA CERRALVO

Yellowfin—Yellowtail

After several years of limited fishing activity in the La Paz area, 1978 showed up to be a banner year, but it had little to do with the fish, per se. It was a modernization of the fishing fleets which made the difference.

As the town grew, the commercial fishing pressures expanded, depleting the stocks of fish close to La Paz that are available to the sportfisherman; and the old charter boats were too slow to go the more distant fishing grounds. But now there are a number of modern boats owned by Jack Velez which cruise at up to 17 knots during an eight hour charter and provide access to the channel between the peninsula and Isla Espiritu Santo and beyond toward Isla Cerralvo.

Now, a winter-spring fishery of yellowtail complements the summer-fall runs of yellowfin tuna which occur to the east of the islands. Additionally, schools of pompano, roosterfish, jack cravalle and billfish move in and out of the area, but not in the numbers found elsewhere in the Cortez.

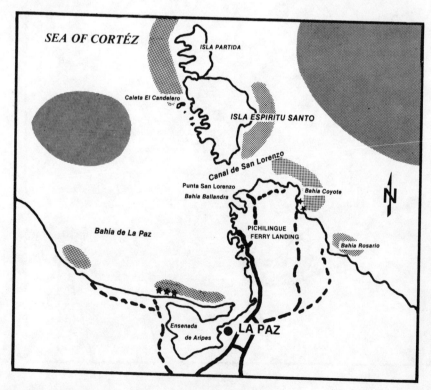

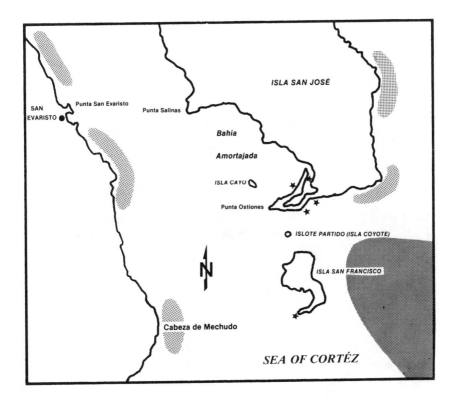

Tuna By The Mile

It was July and I was on my first visit to the islands of San Jose and San Francisco. I had joined Mac and Mary Shroyer of La Paz in their Grand Banks yacht to take pictures for a magazine story. The day was spent taking dorado in the waters south of San Francisco, followed by a snorkeling tour of the beautiful bay. At about 4 p.m. I decided to take my camera and climb to the top of a nearby ridge to shoot down on the anchored boat.

As I looked over the top of the crest I saw such a large mass of birds wheeling and diving that they almost blotted out the horizon. Even at the distance of two miles, I could see the white splashes below. As the mass came closer, the flashing forms of thousands of porpoise became clear. Shortly, about 800 yards, the silvery bodies of tuna became apparent.

Though they were moving rapidly, it took a full 15 minutes for the spectacle to pass in front of me. When they moved toward the horizon I turned to look at the boat and discovered that the light had faded. But the picture I have in my mind today of those miles of tuna is far better than the one I could have taken of the boat in the crystal lagoon.

Zone VII: Loreto-Mulege

Nowhere in the Baja California peninsula does evidence of this finger of land's tumultuous beginnings become so obvious as in the Loreto area. Some 20 million years ago the uneasy writhings of the earth's crust tore loose a huge chunk from the continent and began a slow movement to the northwest. A lifting action formed a high range of mountains along the eastern edge. As the tilting increased and the rift widened, portions tumbled into the sea, forming long undersea ridges and a number of islands. Today it is only a few miles between 6000-foot mountains and great chasms over 1000 fathoms deep. It all adds up to a region which abounds in sealife.

This zone is undoubtedly the most popular destination on the Baja peninsula for the small boater. From October to June the area's many protected beaches and hidden coves are well attended by all manner of trailerable and cartop boats. Campgrounds and hotels too are often crowded with anglers whose tastes lean toward a wide variety of smaller species such as yellowfin tuna, yellowtail, dorado, roosterfish, cabrilla, sierra, etc. Though some marlin and sailfish appear during the summer months, the fishery is not considered great enough for most billfish devotees.

During the winter months there are several locations where the shore caster has an opportunity to toss his lure at schools of yellowtail as they come to within a few feet of shore in pursuit of the *sardinas* which crowd into the coves and along the beaches. Two such areas are just to the north and south of Santa Rosalia. Usually most active as the sun rises, word of their arrival brings hundreds of Mexicans with their handlines and jigs to catch dinner for everyone in town. Beyond the specialized yellowtail fishery, there is an abundance of smaller species which may be taken from the rocky points and along the zone's many beaches. Best times are early and late with small white lures and pieces of bait. A good night time fishery exists near the mouths of the small estuaries in Bahia Concepcion at high tide for pargo, cabrilla and members of the croaker family.

Light winds characterize sheltered campsites throughout the region, but late winter breezes can be stiff and may last three to five days. Hot weather occurs from July through September and temperatures in the 70's and 80's are likely the balance of the year.

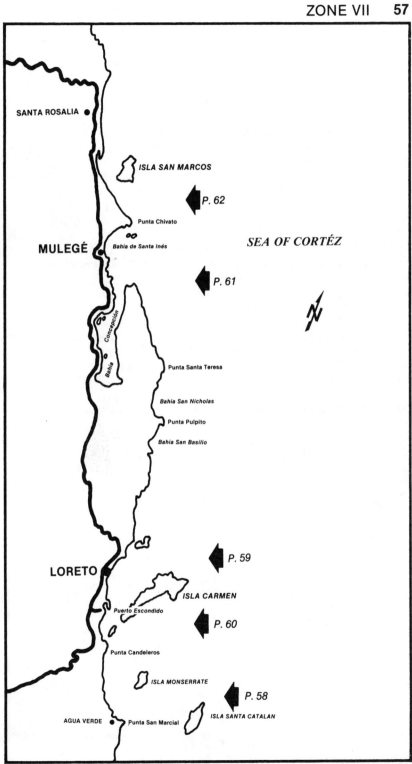

SANTA ROSALIA ●

ISLA SAN MARCOS

P. 62

Punta Chivato

MULEGÉ

Bahia de Santa Inés

SEA OF CORTÉZ

P. 61

Bahia Concepción

Punta Santa Teresa

Bahia San Nicholas

Punta Pulpito

Bahia San Basilio

P. 59

LORETO

ISLA CARMEN

Puerto Escondido

P. 60

Punta Candeleros

ISLA MONSERRATE

P. 58

ISLA SANTA CATALAN

AGUA VERDE ●   Punta San Marcial

Only By Boat

It is unlikely that Bahia Agua Verde and its residents will participate much in the development of the Baja peninsula, but its contributions to the memories of a few small boaters is great.

Located at the back of a well-protected bay, 25 miles south of Puerto Escondido amid a profusion of greenery and palm trees, are the homes of a half-dozen families. Between their small gardens and the abundant fishery just offshore, these resourceful people rarely have to call on the outside world for supplies.

This bay is the best anchorage between La Paz and Loreto, and its numerous coves are a snorkeler's delight. Small members of the bass and snapper families are everywhere providing the best of eating. Seasonally, yellowtail, roosterfish and dorado are found within a few miles of Punta San Marcial.

Bahia Agua Verde is also a jumping-off-place to the island of Santa Catalan, 13 miles to the northeast. Virtually unvisited, it offers predator-free nesting places for a wide variety of birds. The many undersea grottos house a wide variety of sealife for the enjoyment of angler and snorkeler alike.

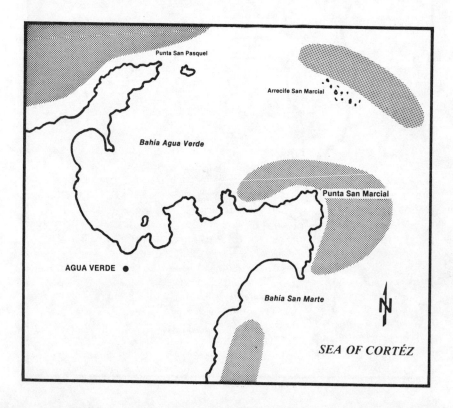

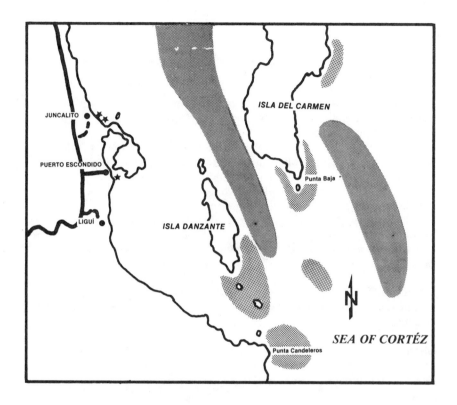

A Winter Haven

As the frost line descends over the Midwest, the motorhomes, campers and house trailers begin arriving in Puerto Escondido and adjacent Juncalito where they set up camp, unload their boats and prepare to wait out the snows in one of the best winter fishing spots in Baja.

Nearby, Isla Danzante and the lower end of Carmen provide plenty of habitat for resident cabrilla, grouper and lesser species and serve as a winter haven for yellowtail and sierra.

On a windy day about ten years ago, I took four kinds of fish in four casts from the pier at Escondido—yellowtail, sierra, amberjack and a beautiful dog snapper weighing almost 25 pounds. The latter forced me to leave the pier and run after it as it headed into the inner bay.

The southern portion of Juncalito is noteworthy because of the schools of small yellowtail which come to within shore casting range a number of times each season. Sometimes the event occurs daily for several weeks; and if one is fortunate enough to be there, he is in for some action.

The Lure of Loreto

For the angler whose sun does not rise and set on the billfish family but looks for the challenge of engaging surface fish on light tackle, the waters around Loreto are hard to beat.

There are almost continual runs of migrating yellowtail, tuna and dorado in the waters of Isla Coronado and the north end of Isla Carmen. The reef between the two islands attracts a constant supply of yellows during the winter and spring, while dorado and yellowfin tuna concentrate outside along the 100 fathom line.

The first part of July usually provides the best fishing anywhere in Mexico for big dorado. Three out of four years that I have been there at that time, nearly everyone was coming in with numerous fish weighing over 40 pounds.

In the late spring, occasional schools of roosterfish enter the area to the north of town along the beach which curves toward Isla Coronado. Shorecasters with large grey or white Straggler Sardine jigs have connected with fish to over 30 pounds. And if you have good legs and a lot of line you may beach one of these babies as much as a half-mile from where you started.

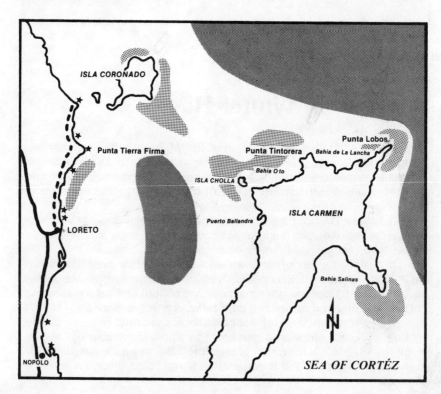

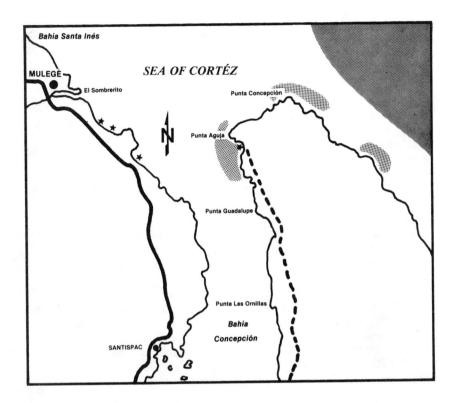

A Popular Bay

Considering the numbers of travelers who now come down the Baja highway, Mulegé has changed little. However, to the south the small coves in Bahia Concepcíon are now trailer camps for many vacationers. Small boats troll offshore for ever-diminishing stocks of sierra, cabrilla and other smaller gamefish. The legend of 100 pound black snook in the brackish waters of the waters of the river at Mulegé still persists; and though many anglers still try for that "big one," I know of no snook larger than about ten pounds that has been taken there in the last ten years.

A very productive destination would be the tip of the peninsula on the opposite side of the bahia. The sandy bottoms and rocky reefs are visited by good numbers of roosterfish, yellowtail and pargo in season. Outside, around the corner into the Cortez, dorado pursue flying fish, half beaks and other edibles in great numbers for much of the summer and fall. Marlin and sailfish also come this far into the gulf.

The beach south and east of the Hotel Serenidad has provided good action on sabalo, sierra, pargo and pompano on several different occasions.

Sierra—The Cibiche Fish

My introduction to the sierra mackerel was at the rocky point just below the now-abandoned Hotel Borrego de Oro at Punta Chivato. We had just completed our walk from the landing strip to the lobby of the hotel when a guest pointed to a furious splashing about 30 yards offshore. In seconds I was off and running with a handful of tackle, assembling it as I went. The sight of the thousands of jumping two-foot silvery fish made my hands shake, but I finally got a lure into the water.

I began the retrieve and felt no resisting tug of the lure or a fish. I reeled in and found the line empty—"Hmm," I thought, "I guess I didn't tie it on well." Another lure, another empty line. And another. "Ah! I need a wire leader." So I tied a bright swivel to the line and cast again. No lure, no wire leader. They were even hitting the shiny swivels! At this rate I was going to be out of tackle before I signed the register.

Then another guest came to my rescue. He gave me several short wire leaders with *black* swivels. The next cast netted me a beautiful four-pound sierra. I took it to the kitchen and an hour later we were enjoying cibiche with our margaritas. A good way to start a weekend.

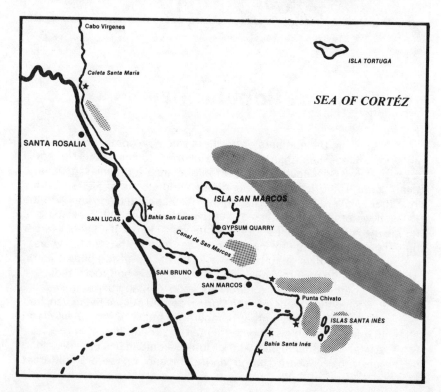

BILL BEEBE

Lesson At Mulege

In the past when the only reasonable access to Mulege was by air, I noticed a well dressed man at the bar of the Serenidad Hotel giving all indications that he was a first-time visitor to Baja. He could be overheard asking what kind of fish was the best to eat because he had promised his family in Nebraska some "biguns" for a fish fry. Our friend bragged that he had bought his tackle from a mail order house and had really saved money, "Fishin' tackle is fishin' tackle." He also couldn't understand why there were no locks on the doors and he obviously had no knowledge of the potency of a Margarita.

The next afternoon the resort's boat brought back a very hostile Nebraskan. He carried two broken rods—one in three pieces—a frozen reel and a 30 yard remnant of his "bargain" line. He notified the desk that he wanted no more of a skipper who couldn't chase the fish quickly enough to keep his gear from coming apart; and he was going home. He blamed everyone except himself.

Later at the bar, one of the regular guests offered to loan him some tackle and take him on his boat. An agreement was made and the next morning the pair departed. When they returned, there were plenty of "biguns" to take home to Nebraska and everything was peaches and cream. He bought a round of drinks and regaled everyone with his new-found fishing expertise.

This man still flys to Baja from Nebraska, and inside his Cessna 210 is some of the most carefully groomed tackle I have ever seen. He learned his lesson.

Zone VIII: The Cortez Midriff

It was not until the recent opening of the 41 mile paved road into Bahia de Los Angeles from the transpeninsular highway that this zone of Baja fishing saw many anglers. Even now the hundreds of miles of productive reefs provide plenty of room for the increased numbers of anglers.

From April to December the key word in the Midriff is action. The strong tidal surges of this narrowest portion of the Sea of Cortez bring cool, nutrient-laden water up from subsurface canyons to mix with warm, oxygen-rich surface waters providing an ideal environment for tremendous blooms of plankton. This in turn creates food for immense populations of small fish which attract yellowtail, sierra mackerel, white seabass, bonito, cabrilla and grouper to name a few. Marlin, dorado and yellowfin tuna are often visitors during the warmest summer months.

Despite the attraction, the Midriff is not without its hazards for the small boater. Heavy winds (especially during November to March) and strong currents which can exceed 10 knots play havoc with fuel consumption, navigation and comfortable boating. Fuel and water are available only at Bahia de Los Angeles and rescue boats do not patrol the area; thus it is safer, and more sensible, to travel with at least one other boat.

Near the southern end of the Midriff Zone at Bahia Santa Teresa the phenomena of finding yellowtail within range of shore casters occurs regularly during the months of October and November. The action usually takes place around dawn and dusk and action on fish ranging upwards of 25 pounds is not uncommon. Elsewhere, and during the balance of the year, the main species taken are cabrilla, spotted sand bass, small grouper, plus an occasional pompano, halibut and sierra. Small white feathers and pieces of shrimp and clams provide the most action. Access to beaches in the Midriff Zone is limited to the area around Bahia de Los Angeles unless you have a vehicle with off-road capabilities. Then you can extend your range to include the areas of Las Animas, San Francisquito and El Barril. Shore fishing in these places is often better because of less angling pressure.

The weather in the Midriff Zone is wide ranging. Winter storms can bring cold winds and heavy rains while the summer months of July, August and September bring heat which often tops 110°F. Wind is a threat any time of the year and a close watch for sudden blows is prudent for boaters. Despite all of the ominous warnings, the Midriff does offer many beautiful days and is a popular Baja destination.

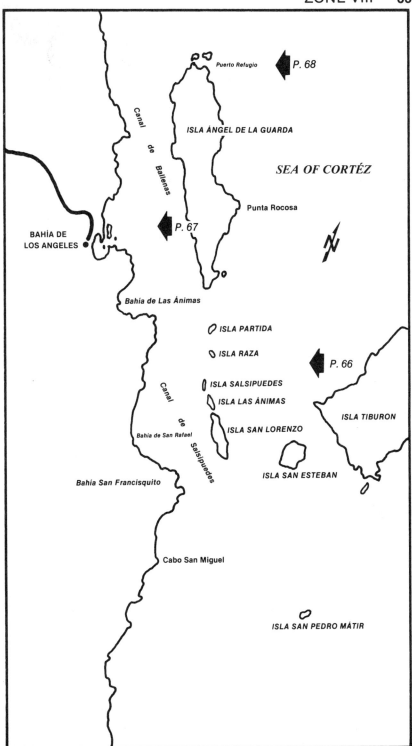

Puerto Refugio

P. 68

Canal   de   Ballenas

ISLA ÁNGEL DE LA GUARDA

SEA OF CORTÉZ

Punta Rocosa

P. 67

BAHÍA DE
LOS ANGELES

Bahía de Las Ánimas

ISLA PARTIDA

ISLA RAZA

P. 66

ISLA SALSIPUEDES

ISLA LAS ÁNIMAS

Canal   de   Salsipuedes

ISLA SAN LORENZO

ISLA TIBURON

Bahía de San Rafael

ISLA SAN ESTEBAN

Bahía San Francisquito

Cabo San Miguel

ISLA SAN PEDRO MÁTIR

Yellowtail Alley

They call it "yellowtail alley," that line of submerged ridges that connects the string of islands from San Lorenzo to Partida. In this area tidal riffs sometimes look like a torrent rushing down a steep canyon. Its action scours up an ideal habitat for almost every form of sealife, from microscopic plankton to huge finback whales—the second largest animal ever to live on this earth.

Grouper, black sea bass, cabrilla and white seabass join the yellows to provide a supreme challenge to any angler who is willing to cast a jig into this maelstrom of life.

Once I joined a group of experienced fishermen to test a spot off the east side of Isla Las Animas for the giant grouper and black sea bass. Though armed with rigs capable of handling up to 100 pound test line, we boated only three fish out of over 100 hookups! And none weighed over 125 pounds.

I have seen yellows erupt over an area of several acres and gorge themselves for an hour or more; and a friend, Tom Payne of Los Angeles, tells of hooking 51 yellowtail in 54 casts without moving the boat.

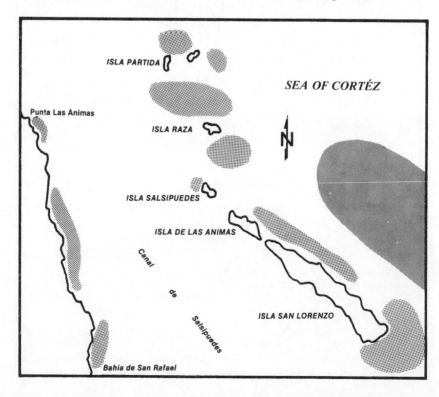

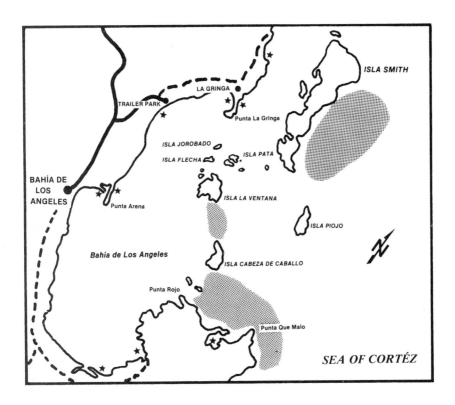

Viva Papa, Viva Mama

One of the most well known couples in Baja are Cruz and Antero Diaz of Bahia de Los Angeles. For more than 25 years they have accommodated a growing number of fly-in visitors along with a scattering of off-roaders who braved the 300 plus miles of miserable roads to experience the challenge of yellowtail, grouper, black sea bass and cabrilla and to partake of their hospitality. Antero supplied the boats and guides, plus an incomparable flair for fun. Any excuse served for a practical joke, the recounting of his adventures, or a fiesta and a serenade on his "kitchen bass." Meanwhile, Cruz performed her kitchen magic for the guest. Her turtle steaks are still the best I've ever eaten. Today, with the opening of paved roads, things are busier than ever.

Seaward, from late April through October, numerous schools of yellowtail join ravenous local residents such as grouper and cabrilla in providing good action. Fishing around Bahia de Los Angeles is subject to the caprice of the winds and the tides. Though it doesn't happen often, the winds can whip the Cortez to a froth in minutes and the strong currents through the channels can exceed 15 knots, so keep a weather eye out and carry extra fuel and water.

Refugio

In my opinion, Puerto Refugio is one of the most interesting spots in the Sea of Cortez. An anchorage safe from almost any quarter, it also is a photogenic combination of multicolored cliffs, islets and pinnacles. One island, Mejia (or Iguana) has large stands of cardon cactus along with numbers of two and a half foot lizards which may be seen sunning themselves or hustling a meal. Another island has a sealion rookery; another serves as a nesting ground for boobys and pelicans. From March through June the area abounds with the young of these and other species.

Much of the year Refugio can satisfy almost any angling desire, as many kinds of fish visit the area to feed on huge shoals of baitfish. The weather is rarely a factor once inside the bay.

On an October visit recently, our boat held over for several days while waiting out one of those Midriff windstorms. Despite gale force winds on the outside there were only light breezes inside where we spent our time taking our fill of yellowtail. As we fished we could hear the wind whistling past the protecting walls of rock.

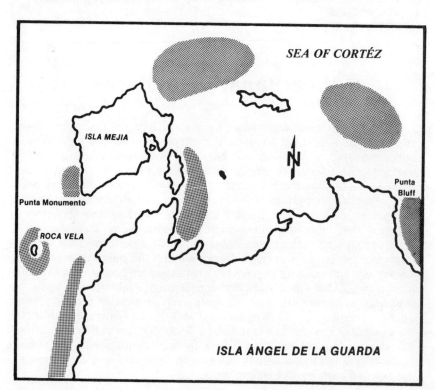

TOM MILLER

Hundreds of pelicans and other seabirds wheeling and diving over boiling yellowtail will give anyone a rapid pulse.

TOM MILLER

Graphic designer Mike Glover called on his fishing skills and competitive instincts to subdue a 70 pound Midriff grouper.

Zone IX: The North Cortez

The nature of the North Cortez fishery off Baja is almost as if it were not connected with the rest of the long gulf. The narrow Midriff and its cooler water acts as a barrier through which few of the species usually associated with warm waters pass. Aside from schools of yellowtail, which stay near the border area between the North Cortez and the Midriff, there appears to be little migratory movement outside the confines of the North Cortez Zone.

Much of the action in this region is keyed to the great tidal variations of the North Cortez. From a three foot difference between high and low at the entrance to the Cortez, the tide surges past the Midriff with an 8.1 foot mean average; by the time it reaches the broad beaches of San Felipe it may exceed 23 feet. Most of the fishing action takes place within two hours of the high tides when the food chain is supplemented by the many crustaceans which live in the tidal plain.

San Felipe offers the closest paved access to the Cortez for the norteamericano. Its mild winter climate draws thousands to the area to fish for plentiful supplies of croaker and corvina. Sierra mackerel are around most of the year but vary widely in numbers from year to year. Within reach of the San Felipe launching spots, white seabass provide good action during the warming days of February to May. Fishing is usually better to the south toward Puertecitos and Bahia Gonzaga; and, though rough in places, many of the unpaved roads are passable to careful drivers.

Shore anglers should plan to fish near the high tides, preferably early or late in the day and at the mouth of an inlet or estero. Small lures and baits (shrimp usually best) can bring corvina, croaker, pompano and spotted sand bass into the beach. If you are lucky enough to have a dune-buggy or wide-tired four-wheel-drive, at least 50 miles of beaches are available. Just bear in mind the high tides when parking or camping.

Summer in this zone can be extremely hot and generally is avoided by tourists, but the balance of the year sees many coming for weekends even for months at a time. Most of the zone's winds come in November through March and may last as much five days, but the calm days more than make up for the inconvenience.

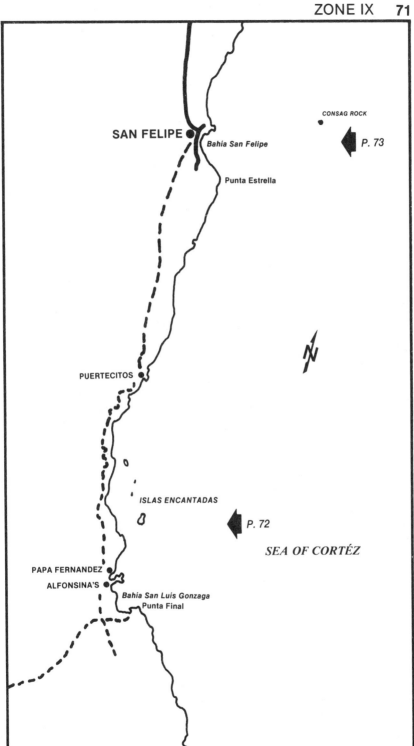

CONSAG ROCK

P. 73

SAN FELIPE

Bahía San Felipe

Punta Estrella

PUERTECITOS

ISLAS ENCANTADAS

P. 72

SEA OF CORTÉZ

PAPA FERNANDEZ

ALFONSINA'S

Bahía San Luís Gonzaga
Punta Final

End Of A Long Trail

There is no place on the Baja peninsula where one can travel over so many bad roads and arrive to find a rather modern motel which serves fine food and has electricity—both a real luxury considering the distance to Alfonsina's Resort from the Baja highway. On the crescent shaped, sandy beach you will see a number of homes and trailers which serve as vacation destinations for Americans.

Once you spend a few days there, you will understand why so many travel so far to visit Bahia Gonzaga and the surrounding area. Miles of shore line provide good fishing for small species such as corvina, pompano, cabrilla, pargo and many others. During the fall and spring, white seabass, grouper and yellowtail trigger good action for small boaters.

Once, while fishing from a rocky point, I caught a small dorado on light tackle. The catch was not much of an accomplishment, but its location and the fact that the month was April made it rather unique.

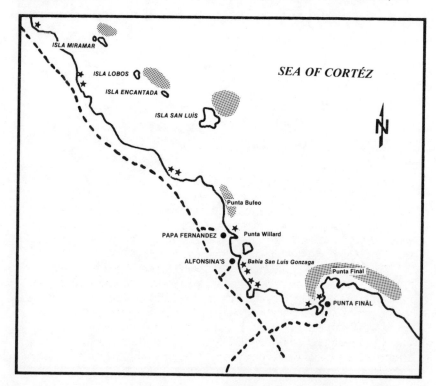

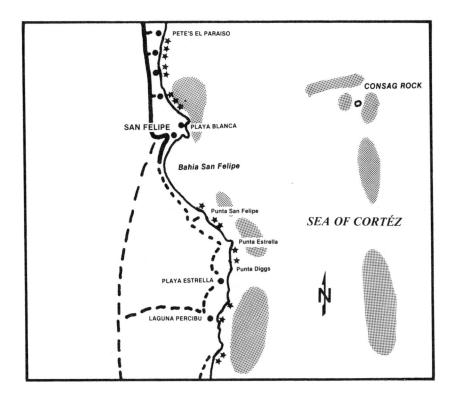

Croaker Country

Fully 90 percent of the catches made in the area of San Felipe are of members of the croaker family, *Sciaenidae*. They include at least three species of corvina, two types of croaker, corbina, white seabass and a scattering of the grandfather of them all, the totuava—whose 200 pound size started the angler's migration toward this dry and dusty fishing village nearly 30 years ago. Currently, the totuava is a protected species that scientists hope will recover from over exploitation.

Twenty miles west-northwest of town Consag Rock is visible on the horizon. Around it are rocky shoals and several channels separated by flat sandy areas. Over these, a wide variety of fish migrate to and from the mouth of the Rio Colorado, 40 miles to the north. Sierra mackerel, corvina and white seabass move in and out over most of the year. Trips to this tall, white rock should not be attempted by the first-time visitor because strong currents and winds can whip up the sea in a hurry. It's best to hire a guide.

Zone X:
The Revillagigedo Archipelago

The most distant of Mexico's island possessions are the three islands of San Benedicto, Socorro and Clarion, plus the twin-spired remnants of an ancient volcano known as Roca Partida. The Revillagigedo Archipelago begins 220 miles south of Cabo San Lucas and extends west-southwest for another 220 miles. Rising abruptly from depths of as much as 2000 fathoms, the upper portions of these seamounts provide habitats for large numbers of tropical gamefish. The islands themselves are uninhabited, save for a small navy garrison on Soccoro.

San Benedicto graphically demonstrates the volcanic origin of the chain of islands. It had a major eruption in 1952 and ashes from the 10,000 foot high plume fell on a ship more than 70 miles distant. For several years scientists watched Benedicto as the smoke and lava continued to spasm through the newly formed cone.

Clarion Island is visited occasionally by naturalists who arrive to study the small animals, the huge populations of sea birds which rise in clouds from their nesting places and the sea turtles who crawl up on the sand to deposit their eggs on the sandy south beach.

All of the islands are visited regularly by tuna boats and large long-range sportfishing boats based in San Diego. The principal target is tuna —yellowfin tuna which surely range over 400 pounds—and there is nowhere in the world where you're more likely to find them.

From November to May, boats on 14 to 16 day cruises arrive almost every week. Each trip is planned to give the angler six to eight days in the area. They are spent trolling or working pinnacles for dorado, wahoo, school-size yellowfin and a host of miscellaneous gamefish. At night the boats anchor and get ready for the big tuna.

After dinner the interest increases as more and more small fish come under the large lights directed into the water. The heavy tackle is baited with a frisky *caballito* and the wait begins. Soon the big resident tuna come up onto the reef from the nearby dropoffs and begin feeding. Huge shadows dart in and out of the lights. The tension grows. Eventually a bait is taken and the battle is on.

The situation is unique, for most of the largest fish taken appear to become disoriented by the lights and the shallow depths around the boat. Several fish of world record caliber have been taken within minutes —even seconds—of when they were hooked. Ordinarily, even a 150 pound yellowfin can strip any reel in seconds, no matter what the line test, if he can get his head in open water. Nowhere else in the world has a yellowfin been taken which topped the 300 pound mark, but thus far 12 over that size have been captured in the Revillagigedo group. So, if you want a big one, you know where to go.

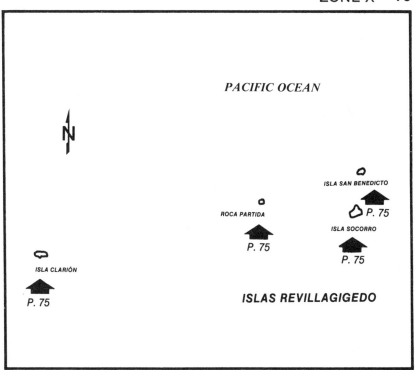

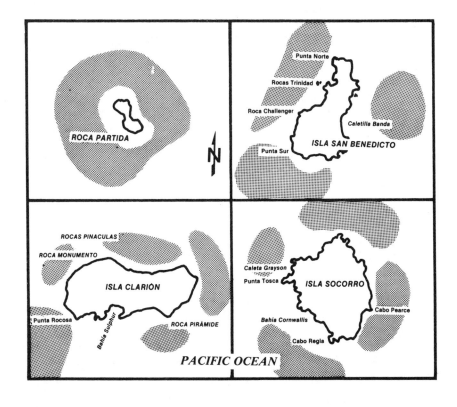

What Is It?

The complex interaction of the many currents, geographical features and climatological conditions around the Baja peninsula provide diverse environments for an astounding variety of fish. Various sources estimate that as many as 1100 types of fish are found in Baja's ten fishing zones. Records also show that at least 200 species have been taken on rod and reel. They range from a one-pound pompano to 1000-pound, and over, blue marlin and all can give a good account of themselves when matching the tackle to the size of the quarry.

Some species are worldwide in range, while others, such as the gulf corvina and the totuava, occur only in Baja waters. To describe and illustrate all of these would take volumes, as there are several dozen more types of fish than are shown in this portion of the book.

A snorkler in the lower Cortez can observe dozens of varieties of reef fish by "baiting" an open spot in a shallow reef. He need only break open a sea urchin, open a few clams, or some other crustacean, and allow it to lay quietly on the bottom. Shortly, there will be a cloud of brightly colored reefdwellers darting from their cover to grab a bite. Attracted by the activity, others approach to watch. Then, as the food is consumed, they all glide back into their protective surroundings.

I have found that almost every extended trip into Baja results in another find which sends me to a reference book in search of a name.

The drawings for this portion of the book were generously supplied from the files of the State of California Department of Fish and Game and augmented with the talented pen of Charles Larson, who drew the additional species not found on the Pacific side of the peninsula. Although the fish classes are shown in general taxonomical order, they are also grouped according to similarities in form or habitat.

The descriptions are brief, but they (in addition to the drawings) provide enough information to identify your catch, at least to family group. English common names and Spanish common names may vary in certain localities, but every effort has been made to minimize the occurrences. The average catch-size of each species is shown, followed by the largest known weight or length to be found in the record books or other sources.

Many of my fellow Baja anglers and myself practice a common sense method of conservation in that, whenever possible, fish, not intended for the dining table, are released unharmed. If this is not possible, every effort is made to see that someone receives the fish in a fresh and healthy condition. In line with this, the descriptions include a short comment on the palatability and suggestions for preparation.

SHARKS and RAYS. More than 60 species are found in the Baja region. Among these are; the largest fish in the world (whale shark), 5 electric rays and strange looking specimens such as the angle shark, horn shark and butterfly ray. Though few resident sharks are considered dangerous, it is always wise to maintain a sharp eye when swimming or diving. Most rays have a poisonous spine on the tail. A sting is rarely fatal but it can be very painful.

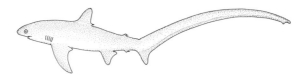

COMMON THRESHER, *Alopias vulpinus*. Tiburon aleta. Common throughout. Offshore-inshore. Tail as long as body. 100-250 lbs., to 700. Takes live and fresh-dead baits. Excellent fighter. Very good eating, prepare like broadbill.

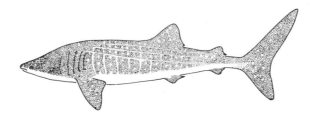

WHALE SHARK, *Rhinocodon typus*. Pez sapo. Magdalena to Midriff, but not common. Offshore. Dark brown above with white spots. 30-45 ft., to 60. A huge, harmless plankton-eater.

SMOOTH HAMMERHEAD, *Sphyrna zygaena*. Cornuda, martillo. Common Magdalena to Midriff, uncommon elsewhere. Offshore-inshore. Grey-brown above, white below. 30-150 lbs., to 500. Takes live and strip baits. Strong fighter. Very good eating, prepare like broadbill.

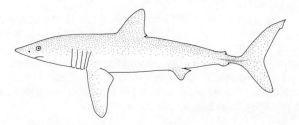

BONITO SHARK, *Isurus oxyrinchus.* **Tiburon, mako.** Widespread but not common. Offshore-inshore. Dark gray above, white below. 25-50 lbs., to 500. Takes live and fresh-dead baits. Excellent fighter. Very good eating, prepare like broadbill.

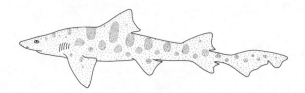

LEOPARD SHARK, *Triakis semifasciata.* **Tiburon.** Common in sandy areas throughout. Onshore. Dark bars on upper body. 2-10 lbs., to 45. Takes clams, crustaceans, dead bait. Makes fast run, then fights doggedly. Good eating.

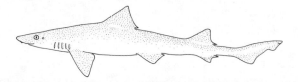

GRAY SMOOTHHOUND, *Mustelus californicus.* **Sand shark.** Common in sandy areas throughout. Onshore. Uniform gray color. 2-5 lbs., to 10. Takes clams, crustaceans, dead bait. Lethargic after first run. Limited food value.

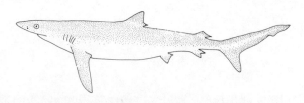

BLUE SHARK, *Prionace glauca.* **Tiburon azul.** Common Pacific to near Cabo. Offshore-inshore. Dark blue above, white below. 30-80 lbs., to 300 + . Takes almost anything dead. Often a pest. Very strong but usually a poor fighter. Meat often has iodine flavor, but edible.

BLACKTIP SHARK, *Carcharhinus limbatus.* **Gambuso.** Magdalena to
Midriff. Offshore-inshore. Tips of fins black. 40-70 lbs., to 125. Live
bait or fresh-dead. Sporty fighter including acrobatics. Popular as
salted, dried meat.

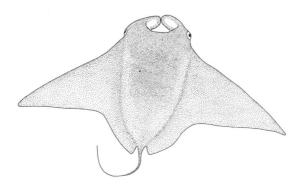

PACIFIC MANTA RAY, *Manta hamiltoni.* **Manta.** Occasional sightings
throughout. Offshore. Black above, white below. Large, to 23 ft.
across and 3500 lbs. Feeds on small organisms. Not a food fish.

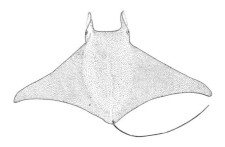

SMOOTHTAIL MOBULA, *Mobula lucasana.* **Manta raya, raya.** Bahia
Tortugas to upper Cortez. Offshore-inshore. Black above, white
below. Travel in groups and often jump pancake-style to 15 ft. in air.
To 4 ft. across. Taken in nets. Meat in wings resembles scallops.

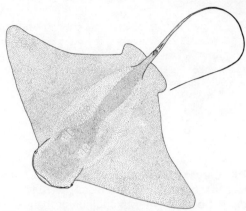

BAT RAY, *Myliobatis californica*. Raya. Common in Pacific, scattered in Cortez. Onshore-inshore. Brown-black above, white below. 20-50 lbs., to 200. Takes clams, crustaceans, squid. Very strong and durable fighter prone to long runs. Meat in wings may be prepared as scallops.

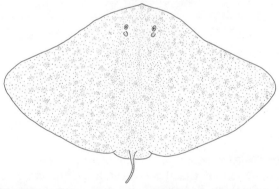

BUTTERFLY RAY, *Gymnura marmorata*. Raya. Common throughout. Inshore-onshore. Brown to olive, often with dark or light spots. 10-20 lbs., to 50. Takes clams, crustaceans, pieces of squid. Food value unknown.

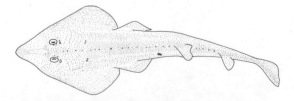

SHOVELNOSE GUITARFISH, *Rhinobatos productus*. Guitarra, shovel-nose shark (not a shark). Common throughout. Onshore. Brown above, white below, nose translucent. 3-10 lbs., to 40. Takes clams, crustaceans, dead bait. Sluggish fighter. Round fillet from tail may be prepared as scallops.

SILVERY FISHES. The 50 or more species of these fishes all have a similarity in appearances and habits—they are of a silvery color and most gather in schools. This group comprises the most important supply of forage fishes for the popular game species. Many are used as live or dead bait.

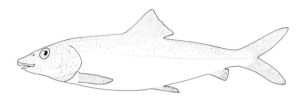

BONEFISH, *Albula vulpes.* **Quijo, sabalo.** Common in shallow estuaries from Laguna Manuela to above La Paz. Inshore-onshore. Brownish-silver above, white below, prominent scales. 1-3 lbs., to 10. Takes clams, crustaceans, small baits. So-so fighter, not like in Atlantic. Makes excellent live bait for roosterfish. Limited food value.

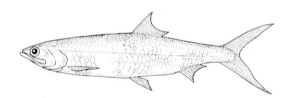

LADYFISH, *Elops affinis.* **Sabalo, machete.** Common Magdalena to La Paz. May range further north. Inshore-onshore. Silvery body. 1-3 lbs., to 8. Takes small lures or live sardinas. Excellent fighter with acrobatics. Very bony flesh.

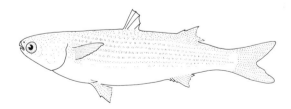

STRIPED MULLET, *Mugil cephalus.* **Lisa. Liseta.** Common throughout in bays, estuaries and protected waters. Onshore. Silvery with dark stripes, broad snout. 6-18 inches, to 30. Taken in nets or snagged for bait. Fair food fish.

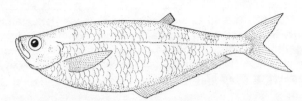

HERRINGS, Family Clupeidae. *Sardina.* There are many species similar in shape. Common Magdalena and throughout Cortez. Inshore-onshore. Bluish above, silvery below with prominent scales. To 6 in. Important as forage and bait fish.

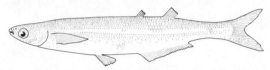

CALIFORNIA GRUNION, *Leuresthes tenuis.* Grunion. Common on Pacific side south to about Magdalena. Greenish above, silvery sides. To 7 in. Spawn on beaches on night high tides. Tasty when fried. A daylight-spawning species, ***L. sardina,*** is found in northern Cortez.

ELONGATED FISHES. About 30 species. In appearance they have long thin bodies, plus individual adaptations for survival such as; elongated and enlarged fins (flying fishes), long, sharp jaws (needle-fishes) or transluscent bodies (halfbeaks).

MEXICAN NEEDLEFISH, *Strongylura fodiator.* Agujon. Several other species found throughout, but this largest species occurs from Cabo north to Midriff. Offshore-inshore. Bluish above, silvery below. Teeth and bones are green. 2-4 ft., to 6. Takes fast-trolled feathers and drifted sardinas. Good fighter, wild acrobat. Excellent eating. Flesh is greenish but turns white when cooked.

HALFBEAKS, Family Hemiramphidae. Pajarito. Found throughout but most common in Cortez to Midriff. Offshore-inshore. Blue-green above, silvery below. Note lower jaw. To 18 in. Important forage fish.

CORNETFISH, *Fistularia commersonii*. Corneta. Common in southern portions of Cortez. Onshore. Brownish above, lighter below. Can change color in water to match background. Note skull extension with mouth at end. 1½ ft., to nearly 3. Takes small baits or lures cast around rocks. Fair fighter. Edible.

FLYINGFISHES, Family Exocoetidae. **Pez volador.** Common throughout. At least 4 species. Blue above, silvery below. Note pectoral fins. To 16 in. Important forage fish.

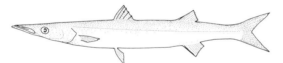

CALIFORNIA BARRACUDA, *Sphyraena argentea*. Picuda agujon. Pacific to Cabo. A smaller species, **S. ensis,** found in Cortez. Bluish-brown above, silvery below with sharp teeth. 2-5 lbs., to 14. Hits jigs readily, also live bait. Fair fighter. Good food fish.

BOTTOM DWELLERS. More than 100 species not covered elsewhere are considered to prefer depths of 100 feet and more. Most are kept for use as food or bait. A majority are reddish in color with large heads and sharp spines.

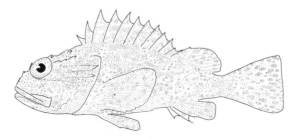

SCULPIN, *Scorpaena guttata*. Scorpionfish. Pacific south to almost Magdalena. Inshore. Red to brown with dark spots. Spines are mildly poisonous. 1-2 lbs., to 4. Takes baits and lures bounced off bottom. Little fight. Meat is excellent.

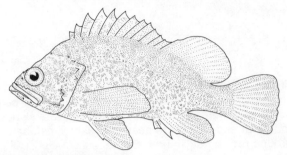

ROCKFISH, Genus Sebastes. Kelp rockfish illustrated is typical of more than 40 species found south to Magdalena. Inshore. Most are reddish with variations of bars, spots, etc. 1-30 lbs. Takes baits and lures bounced off bottom. Little fight. Meat is highly prized.

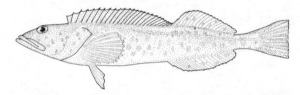

LINGCOD, *Ophiodon elongatus.* Coronado Islands to Punta San Carlos (below El Rosario). Inshore. Color varies from brown to greenish to bluish. 3-10 lbs., to 40. Takes squid, anchovies and larger jigs bounced off bottom. Strong fighter having an exasperating tendency to hold bait in teeth, then release. Excellent eating.

BASSES. The over 30 species vary widely in size, ranging from 1000-pound jewfish to a 4-ounce sand perch. All are predators and very good eating. Most live in the rocks.

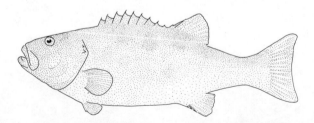

GIANT SEA BASS, *Stereolopis gigas.* Black sea bass, mero prieto, pescaro. Fairly common in rocky areas below San Quintin to above Midriff in Cortez. Inshore. Dark gray-brown. 30-200 lbs., to over 500. Takes, 1-4 lb. whole or chunk baits held near rocky bottom. Very strong, dogged fighter. Excellent eating.

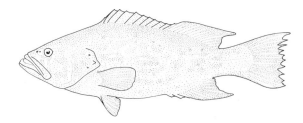

BROOMTAIL GROUPER, *Mycteroperca xenarcha.* **Garropa, jasplada.**
Cedros to Midriff. Not common anywhere. Inshore. Gray, often with
brown markings. 10-25 lbs., to 80. Takes large baits and jigs. Strong
fighter, dives into rocks. Superb eating.

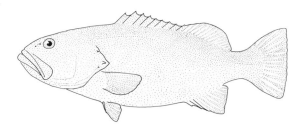

GULF GROUPER, *Mycteroperca jordani.* **Baya, garropa astillero.** Alijos
Rocks to above Midriff. Inshore. Brown above, gray below. 25-100
lbs., to 200. Large baits and jigs. Very strong fighter, dives into
rocks. Superb eating.

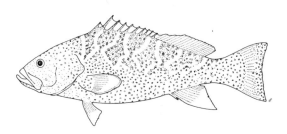

LEOPARD GROUPER, *Mycteroperca rosacea.* **Cabrilla pinto.** Alijos
Rocks to near San Felipe. Inshore. Brown with many small black
spots. There is also a gold colored phase called **golden grouper** or
calamaria. 5-25 lbs., to 50. Smaller baits and jigs. Good fighter,
using rocks to advantage. First-class eating.

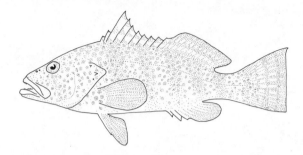

SPOTTED CABRILLA, *Epinephelis analogus.* **Pinta cabrilla, cabrilla.**
Cedros Islands to near San Felipe. Abundant in rocks from Midriff
to Cabo San Lucas. Inshore. Reddish brown with dark spots over
body and fins. 3-10 lbs., to 30. Readily hits feathers, jigs and fresh-
dead sardinas. Good fighter using rocks to advantage. Considered
the finest of eating, fried, or raw in cebiche.

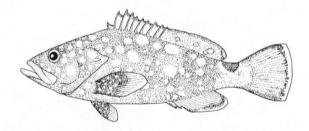

FLAG CABRILLA, *Epiniphelus labriformis.* **Cabrilla.** Common in rocky
shallows in Cortez from Cabo to Midriff. Inshore-onshore. Dark
reddish-green body with white spots and white margins on fins. 1-2
lbs., Takes small baits and crustaceans and will hit small jigs. Use
as live bait for grouper, also very good eating.

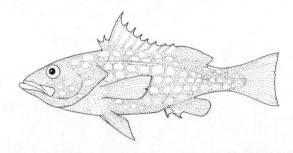

GOLDSPOTTED BASS, *Paralabrax auroguttatus.* **Cabrilla pintado,**
extranjero. Common throughout Cortez and to at least Magdalena.
Inshore. Light olive brown with golden spots over body and fins. To
2 lbs. Takes small baits near bottom or yoyo'd jigs. Excellent live
bait and food fish.

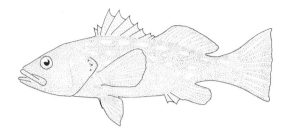

KELP BASS, *Paralabrax clathratus*. Cabrilla. Common in the kelp beds from border to Cedros. Inshore-onshore. Yellow-brown to brown with whitish blotches and black spots on back. 1-5 lbs., to 14. Takes live baits, squid, mussels and jigs. Good food fish.

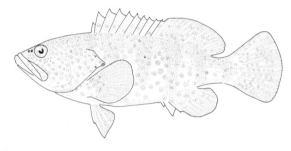

SPOTTED SAND BASS, *Paralabrax maculatofasciatus*. Spotted bay bass, cabrilla pintica. Common border to Magdalena. Uncommon lower Cortez, abundant upper Cortez. Inshore-onshore. Olive-brown with many small black spots. 1-3 lbs., Takes live baits, small baits and hits feathers. Good live bait and very good eating.

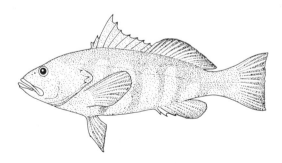

BARRED SAND BASS, *Paralabrax nebulifer*. Sand bass, cabrilla. Common border to Magdalena. Inshore-onshore. Gray with dark bars on sides. 1-5 lbs., to 10. Takes live baits, squid and jigs bounced along sandy bottom. Prized for eating.

DORADO, MACKERELS and TUNAS. The 12 or so species are noted for their powerful, streamlined bodies which provide the ability to move rapidly through the water. All are predators and migrate widely. The wahoo is believed to be one of the fastest of fishes— over 50 mph. Almost all are prized gamefish.

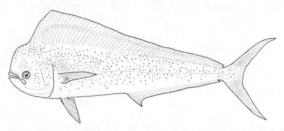

DORADO, *Coryphaena hippurus*. Dolfinfish, mahi mahi. Wide ranging throughout, most common Magdalena to Mulege. Offshore-inshore. Changes color rapidly—blue to green above, sides yellow with blue and green spots, white below. 7-40 lbs., to 70. Hits lures, live bait and trolled dead bait. Good fighter with lots of acrobatics. Meat is prized when fresh.

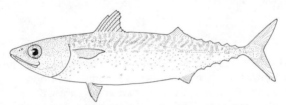

PACIFIC MACKEREL, *Scomber japonicus*. Greenback, makerela. Throughout Pacific, less common in Cortez. Offshore-inshore. Green above with dark wavy lines, silvery below. 1-2 lbs., to 5. Mackerel jigs, small feathers or small baits. Good fighter and excellent bait, live or dead. Meat oily but good smoked.

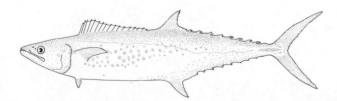

SIERRA, *Scomberomorus sierra*. Pez sierra. From Cedros, south and throughout Cortez. Inshore. Dark blue back, balance silvery with yellowish spots on sides. 1-5 lbs., to 15. Hits jigs and live bait. A good fighter with very sharp teeth. Superb eating, especially as cibiche. Also good bait, whole or cut.

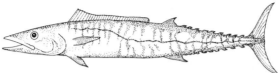

WAHOO, *Acanthocybium solandri.* **Sierra golfina.** Magdalena to Cabo and to area of Cerralvo. Offshore-inshore. Dark blue above fading to silver below with dark bars which flash blue when alive. 20-50 lbs., to 110. Fast trolled large jigs and live bait. An excellent fighter with screaming runs. Superb eating.

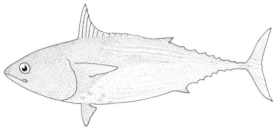

BLACK SKIPJACK, *Euthynnus lineatus.* **Barrilete.** Common Magdalena to upper Cortez. Offshore-inshore. Dark above, silvery below, stripes on back and 3 or 4 black spots on forward abdomen. 3-8 lbs., to 12. Hits cast and trolled jigs, live bait. Strong, fast fighter. Good bait, but meat very strong flavored.

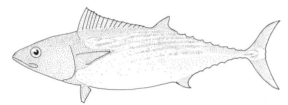

PACIFIC BONITO, *Sarda chiliensis.* **Bonito.** Common throughout to Midriff. Offshore-inshore. Dark blue above, silvery below with oblique lines on back. 2-8 lbs., to 20. Hits jigs, live bait. Strong fighter. Good eating, especially if fillets are marinated and barbequed. Also good bait.

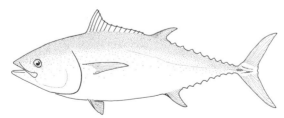

BLUEFIN TUNA, *Thunnus thynnus.* **Atun.** Common to Cedros, uncommon to Cabo San Lucas. Inshore-offshore. Deep blue above, silvery below with short pectoral fins. 15-40 lbs., to 200. Hits lively anchovies, occasionally trolled jigs. Strong fighter with speedy first run. Prized raw for sashimi, also good cooked.

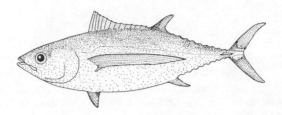

ALBACORE, *Thunnus alalunga*. Aibacora. Pacific south to Guadalupe Island. Offshore-inshore. Gray-black above, silver-gray below with long pectoral fins. 5-25 lbs., to 45. Readily strikes trolled jigs and live bait. Strong fighter, highly sought. Excellent eating, especially canned or smoked.

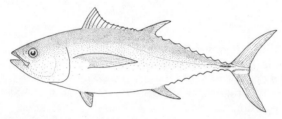

YELLOWFIN TUNA, *Thunnus albacares*. Atun de aleta amarilla, albacora. Throughout to Midriff. Offshore-inshore. Dark blue above, silver below with yellow-tinged fins and finlets. 15-100 lbs, to 400+. Strikes trolled jigs and live bait. Very powerful fighter with great durability. Excellent food fish, especially canned and smoked.

JACKS. The 27 species of jacks are predators, feeding on smaller fishes, squid, etc. Most frequent inshore waters and are pelagic. They vary in desirability as food from excellent (pompano) to not much (roosterfish). All are highly regarded as gamefish.

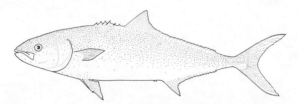

YELLOWTAIL, *Seriola dorsalis*. Jurel, jurel de aleta amarilla. Common throughout except far north in Cortez. Inshore-onshore (at times). Blue-gray to olive above with yellow stripe along side, fins yellowish. 5-25 lbs., to 60. Takes drifted chunk or strip bait, live bait or jigs, trolled, cast and yoyo'd. A superb adversary. Best when fillets are marinated and barbequed.

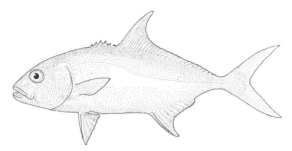

PACIFIC AMBERJACK, *Seriola colburni.* **Pez fuerte.** Occurs south of Cedros to Midriff, commonest Cabo to Loreto. Inshore. Bronze above, cream to yellow below. 5-80 lbs., to 150+. Taken on jigs and live bait. A strong fighter which can strip your reel of line. Good when filleted and barbequed.

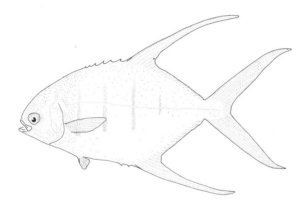

GAFFTOPSAIL POMPANO, *Trachinotis rhodopis.* **Pompanito.** Magdalena to above Midriff. Inshore. Silver-gray above, silver below with yellow to bronze fins. 1-5 lbs. Hard to take on lures but do hit small live baits. Durable fighters when hooked. Very good eating.

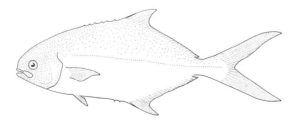

PANCAKE POMPANO, *Trachinotis kennedyi.* **Palometa.** From Magdalena and throughout Cortez. Inshore-onshore. Silver-gray above, silver below. 1-10 lbs., to 40. Smaller ones taken from shore on small white feathers, lures; adults found in shallows and take live bait, occasional jig. Good fighter, including acrobatics. Excellent eating.

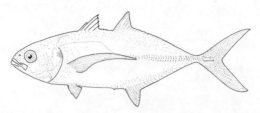

GREEN JACK, *Caranx caballus.* **Caballito, cocinero.** Magdalena to Cabo and into southern Cortez. Inshore. Greenish-bronze above dusky below. 8-12 in., to 20. Taken on mackerel jigs or small lures and baits. Principal value is as live bait for billfish, tuna.

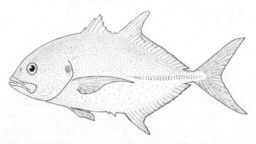

JACK CREVALLE, *Caranx caninus* (also identified as *C. hippos*). **Toro.** Magdalena and throughout Cortez, but most common La Paz to Cabo. Inshore-onshore. Silver-gray above with black spots on gill-cover and pectoral fin. 3-25 lbs., to 50. Taken on jigs and live baits. A tough and mobile fighter. Only fair eating as meat is strong and dark.

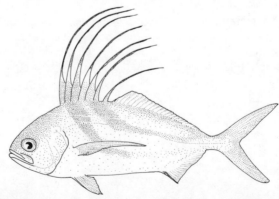

ROOSTERFISH, *Nematistius pectoralis.* **Pez gallo, papagallo.** Magdalena and throughout Cortez. Inshore-onshore. Gray above, silver below with two pronounced diagonal stripes. 20-50 lbs., to 100 + . Commonly taken on live bait, rarely on jigs. One of the top fighters found in Baja with slashing moves and long runs. Meat is very dark, used in stews, etc.

MEXICAN LOOKDOWN, *Selene brevoorti.* **Chopeta, luna.** Magdalena to Cabo and lower Cortez. Inshore. Bluish-green above, sides silvery. 1-2 lbs. Takes small baits and small feathers. Fair fighter. Very good eating.

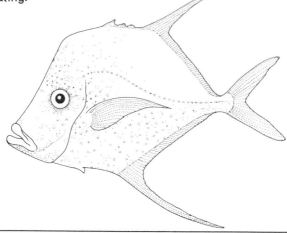

CORVINAS and CROAKERS. Most of the 30 or so species are plentiful throughout the range and comprise a large portion of the light tackle, small game fishing. The corvinas feed principally on small fishes and have some teeth, while the croakers usually are found grubbing around on sandy bottoms for crustaceans, worms, etc. as they have few teeth. All make croaking sounds. *NOTE—It is not legal to take or possess totuava.*

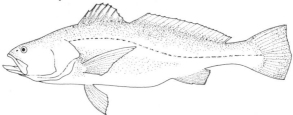

TOTUAVA, *Cynoscion macdonaldi.* **Totoaba, totuava.** Found only in upper Cortez and currently not plentiful. Inshore. Coppery-gray above, shading to silver-gray. 35-100 lbs., to 250. Takes live croaker baits and hits large yoyo'd white jigs. Makes strong first run, then fair fighter. Considered one of the finest eating fish anywhere.

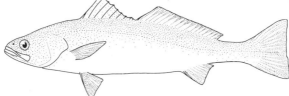

WHITE SEABASS, *Cynoscion nobilis.* **Corvina blanca.** North of Magdalena, Midriff and upper Cortez. Inshore. Bluish-gray above shading to silver below with ridge along belly. 10-40 lbs., to 80. Takes squid and readily hits yoyo'd white and chrome jigs. Strong first run, then dogged fighter. Excellent eating.

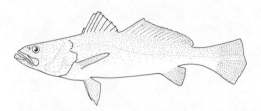

ORANGEMOUTH CORVINA, *Cynoscion xanthulus*. Corvina de aletas amarillas. In Magdalena area and throughout Cortez, most common above Midriff. Inshore-onshore. Bluish-gray above to silver overall; tail and fins yellowish. Inside of mouth a bright orange. 2-10 lbs., to 30. Takes squid, crustaceans, live bait and readily hits jigs and feathers. Fair fighter. Excellent eating.

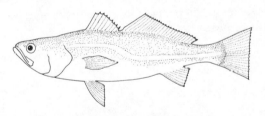

GULF CORVINA, *Cynoscion othonopterus*. Golfina. Upper portion of Cortez only. Inshore-onshore. Silver with bluish cast and larger scales. 5-15 lbs., to 20. Takes jigs readily and probably shrimp and live bait. Fair fighter. Excellent eating.

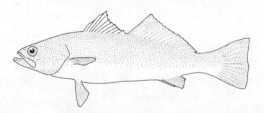

SHORTFIN CORVINA, *Cynoscion parvipinnis*. Corvina pacifico, corvina azul. Scammon's Lagoon south and all of Cortez. Inshore-onshore. Bluish-gray above shading to silver. With prominent canine teeth in upper jaw. 2-10 lbs. Takes small jigs and crustacean baits, also live baits. Fair fighter. Excellent eating.

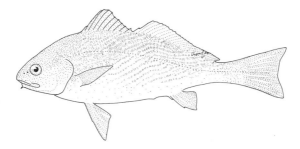

YELLOWFIN CROAKER, *Umbrina roncador.* **Roncador.** Throughout area. Onshore. Grayish with brown-black wavy lines on side, fins yellowish. 1-4 lbs. Takes shellfish, crustaceans and small live baits. Spirited fighter. Very good eating.

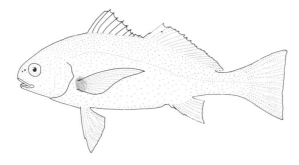

SPOTFIN CROAKER, *Roncador stearnsii.* **Roncador.** To Magdalena, also reported in Cortez. Onshore. Gray to brassy above shading to white, with black spot at base of pectoral. 2-6 lbs., to 12. Takes shellfish, crustaceans. Prized quarry for surf fishermen, good fighter. Excellent eating.

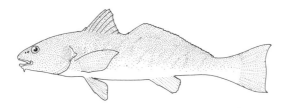

CALIFORNIA CORBINA, *Menticirrhus undulatus.* **Corbina, corvina.** Throughout, but common south to Magdalena and in upper Cortez. Onshore. Gray-blue above shading to white or silver below. 1-4 lbs., to 7. Takes shellfish, crustaceans. Good fighter. Excellent eating.

SURF FISHES. At least 6 families and 25 species are taken almost exclusively by the surf angler. Most are found on the Pacific side of the peninsula. They dig in the sand for crustaceans and worms or nibble mosses and small bivalves from the rocks.

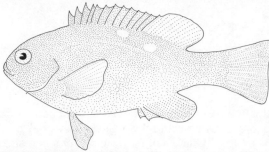

OPALEYE, *Girella nigricans*. Ojo azul. To at least Magdalena. Closely related **G. simplicidens** is found in upper Cortez. Onshore in rocky areas. Dark olive-green with two light spots near dorsal (other has three) and bright blue-green eyes. 1-4 lbs., to 8 + . Takes mussels, green moss, green peas. Fair fighter. Fair eating—at times tastes of iodine.

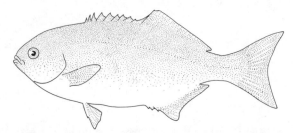

HALFMOON, *Medialuna californiensis*. Catalina perch, blueperch. Pacific to at least Magdalena. Onshore in rocky areas. Dark blue above, lighter blue below. 1-2 lbs., to 4. Takes shellfish, small baits. Good fighter. Fair eating.

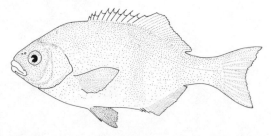

RUBBERLIP SURFPERCH, *Rhacochilus toxotes*. Buttermouth perch. Pacific to Bahia Tortugas. Onshore in rocky areas. Brassy-brown above, tan below with large yellowish lips. 1-2 lbs. Takes shellfish, bloodworms. Fair fighter. Very good eating.

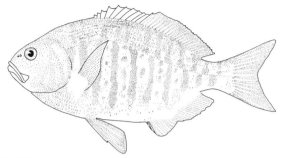

BARRED SURFPERCH, *Amphistichus argenteus.* **Barred perch.** Pacific to near Morro Santo Domingo. Onshore in sandy areas. Olive to gray on back, silver sides with dark bars. 1-2 lbs., to 4. Takes variety of baits including crustaceans, shellfish and salted anchovies. Good fighter. Excellent eating.

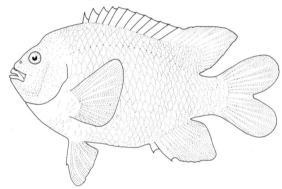

GARIBALDI, *Hypsypops rubicundus.* **Golden perch.** Pacific to Magdalena. Onshore in rocky areas. Brilliant orange over all 1-2 lbs. A beautiful fish which should be released if caught incidently.

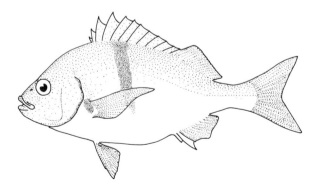

SARGO, *Anisotremus davidsonii.* **Sargo, rayado.** North of Magdalena and in upper Cortez. Inshore-onshore. Gray above shading to white with black bar. 1-5 lbs. Takes clams, crustaceans, usually around rocks. Fair fighter. Good tablefare.

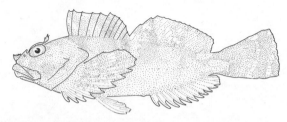

CABEZON, *Scorpaenichthys marmoratus*. Common to San Quintin but found to Punta Abreojos. Onshore-inshore. Reddish to greenish with dark spots and soft pelvic and dorsal spines. 2-4 lbs., to 15. Takes mussels, squid, anchovies. Fair fighter, often diving into rocks or kelp. Excellent eating, but roe (eggs) is **poisonous.**

BILLFISHES. 6 species are found around Baja. All are prized for their fighting ability and, often, spectacular acrobatics. Other than the swordfish, the palatibility is questionable. Those taken should be released.

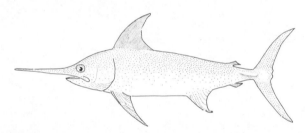

SWORDFISH, *Xiphias gladius*. Broadbill, pez espada. Pacific to Cabo, occasionally in Cortez. Offshore. Body black above, gray below, with flattened bill and no pelvic fins. 125-350 lbs., to 800. Takes live bait, even bonito, also giant squid and large dead baits. Described as the ultimate tough fighter, it rarely jumps. Excellent steaked and broiled.

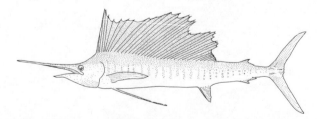

SAILFISH, *Istiophorus platypterus*. Pez vela. Occurs throughout but common from Magdalena to Midriff. Offshore-inshore. Purple-blue above with light blue bars, silvery below. 50-100 lbs., to 175. Taken trolling jigs or flying fish, also live bait. A good and very acrobatic fighter. Poor food value.

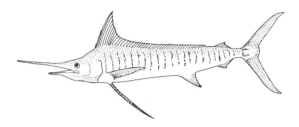

STRIPED MARLIN, *Tetrapturus audax*. Marlin. Occurs Pacific to Midriff. Offshore. Purple-brown above with light blue bars, silver-gray below. 100-175 lbs., to 350. Taken trolling jigs or flying fish, also live bait. A strong, acrobatic fighter. Fair food value.

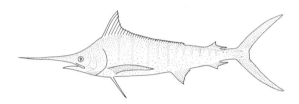

BLUE MARLIN, *Makaira nigricans*. Marlin azul. Common Magdalena to La Paz, rare elsewhere. Offshore. Dark blue above, silver below with dark bars on sides—pectoral fins can be folded back along sides. 250-500 lbs., to 1100. Taken trolling jigs or flying fish, also live bait. Tough, durable fighter, does little jumping. Fair food fish.

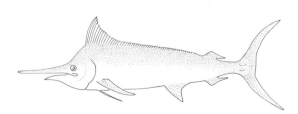

BLACK MARLIN, *Makaira indica*. Marlin negro. Occurs Magdalena to La Paz, rare elsewhere. Offshore. Dark blue above, silver below with *no* bars—pectoral fins cannot be folded back. 200-400 lbs., to 800. Taken trolling jigs or flying fish, also live bait. Tough, durable fighter, does little jumping. Fair food fish.

FLATFISHES. Around 35 species are represented. All have both eyes on one side of their head. In size they range from an 8-inch tongue-fish to the California halibut which exceeds 40 lbs. Almost all bear the Spanish name, *Lenguado.*

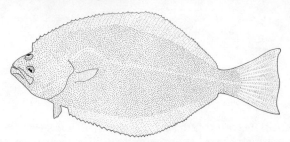

CALIFORNIA HALIBUT, *Paralichthys californicus.* **Lenguádo.** Pacific to Magdalena, isolated population in upper Cortez. Inshore-onshore. Dark brown above, white below. 3-10 lbs., to 40. Drifted small live or dead baits, small feathers. Fair fighter with tender mouth. Excellent food fish.

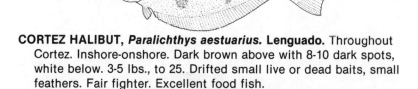

CORTEZ HALIBUT, *Paralichthys aestuarius.* **Lenguado.** Throughout Cortez. Inshore-onshore. Dark brown above with 8-10 dark spots, white below. 3-5 lbs., to 25. Drifted small live or dead baits, small feathers. Fair fighter. Excellent food fish.

WRASSES and PARROTFISHES. At least 25 species of these two families brighten up the seas around Baja. Most are colorful and many are small, but their general habitat around shallow reefs make them highly visible. Several of the larger members make fine eating.

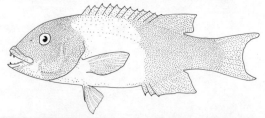

CALIFORNIA SHEEPHEAD, *Pimelometopon pulchrum.* Pacific to Cabo, at Midriff in Cortez. Inshore. Male, black, red and black; female, uniform brownish-red. Both have white chin. 3-10 lbs., to 40. Squid, live bait, also yoyo'd jigs. Good fighter. Excellent and versatile food fish.

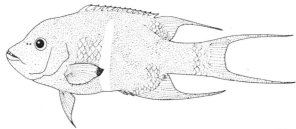

MEXICAN HOGFISH, *Bodianus diplotaenia.* **Vieja.** Above Magdalena to above Midriff. Inshore. Dark blue-green body with yellow bar; fins often purplish, big scales. 3-6 lbs., to 20. Takes bait and occasionally yoyo'd jigs. Good fighter. Edible but usually released because of their beauty.

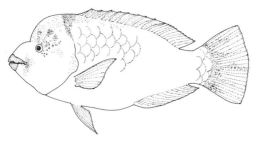

BUMPHEAD PARROTFISH, *Scarus perrico.* **Perico, guacamaya.** Magdalena to Mulege. Inshore-onshore. Body bluish-green, fins darker blue, large scales. 5-10 lbs., to 30. Difficult to hook, try small pieces of crestaceans or squid. Fair fighter. Good steamed in salads or barbequed whole.

SNAPPERS. There are 9 species which range from Magdalena into the Cortez. They feed mainly at night on small fishes and crustaceans. Widely sought for sport and food. Most turn reddish when dead.

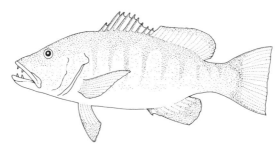

DOG SNAPPER, *Lutjanus novemfasciatus.* **Pargo prieto, boca fuerte.** Laguna San Ignacio south and throughout Cortez. Inshore. Reddish body with darker bars and large canine teeth on both jaws. 5-25 lbs., to 85. Takes live bait and jigs. Good fighter. Very good eating.

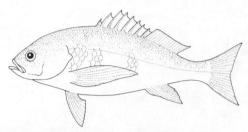

RED SNAPPER, *Lutjanus peru.* **Huachinango.** Magdalena to Cabo and throughout Cortez. Inshore. Body and fins bright red, belly pink to white. 2-5 lbs., to 15. Takes baits near bottom and yoyo'd jigs. Fair fighter. Superb eating.

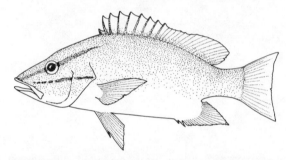

YELLOW SNAPPER, *Lutjanus argentiventris.* **Pargo amarillo.** Magdalena to Cabo and through Cortez. Inshore. Golden-yellow, sometimes reddish on belly and head; black line through eye, blue line below eye. 2-8 lbs., to 20. Night feeder, takes squid, crustaceans and chunk baits. Good fighter. Good eating.

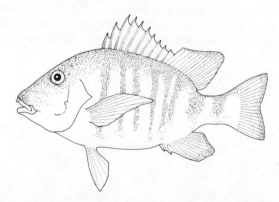

BARRED PARGO, *Hoplopagrus guntheri.* **Striped pargo, pargo mulato.** Magdalena to Cabo and throughout Cortez. Inshore-onshore. Greenish-bronze on back, reddish below with about 8 dark bars. 3-10 lbs., to 25. Hits chunks of bait on bottom. Very good fighter. Very good eating.

MISCELLANEOUS and ODDBALLS. These fish do not fit into the categories on the preceding pages. The list is limited only by space for there are many strange and unusual species to be seen in Baja waters. The first 5 fish are of food or bait value, the balance are merely curiosities which are common.

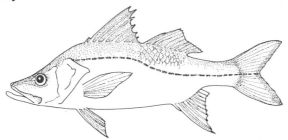

BLACK SNOOK, *Centropomus nigrescens*. Robalo, robalo prieto. Laguna San Ignacio to Mulege. Inshore-onshore. Bluish above, silver below with prominent dark lateral line. 2-10 lbs., to 40 + . Takes small live mullet, some jigs. Good fighter. Excellent eating.

FINESCALE TRIGGERFISH, *Balistes polylepis*. Cochi, puerco. Common below Abreojos, abundant throughout Cortez. Inshore-onshore. Brownish body, sometimes with small blue spots, powerful teeth. 2-4 lbs., to 8. Will take almost any bait, most jigs, voracious. Strong, stubborn fighter. Very good eating, meat has crab-like flavor.

ORANGESIDE TRIGGERFISH, *Sufflamen verres*. Cochi. Common in lower Cortez, reported to Magdalena. Inshore-onshore. Brownish with orange sides, brighter on males. 1-2 lbs. Will take almost any bait, small jigs, voracious. Stubborn fighter. Good eating with crab-like flavor.

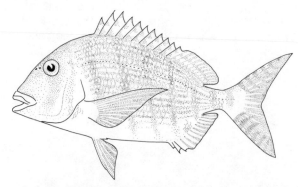

PACIFIC PORGY, *Calamus brachysomus*. Mojarra grabata. Throughout, but most common in upper Cortez. Inshore-onshore. Reddish-green above with dark bars, silver to gray below. 1-5 lbs. Takes clams, crustaceans in shallow rocky areas. Fair fighter. Good tablefare.

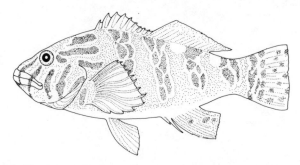

CROWN HAWKFISH, *Cirrhitus rivulatus*. Chino mero, pargo tigre. Magdalena to upper Cortez. Inshore-onshore. Brownish body with blue-edged irregular black markings similar in appearance to Chinese writing. 1-4 lbs. Takes small baits and crustaceans; rarely a jig. Good fighter. Very good eating.

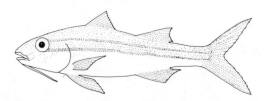

GOATFISH, *Pseudupeneus grandisquamis*. Chivo, barbon. Magdalena to Mulege, common from La Paz to Cabo. Inshore-onshore. Greenish back with yellow body stripes. To 18 inches. Takes minute baits or are netted for use as baitfish. Presumably edible, but makes good, durable bait.

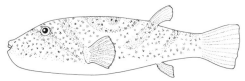

BULLSEYE PUFFER, *Sphoeroides annulatus.* **Bolete.** Common
Magdalena throughout Cortez. Inshore-onshore. Body brown with
black spots and bullseye pattern on back. Puffs up like a balloon
when molested. 1-3 lbs. Takes anything; a pest. Poor fighter.
Poisonous, do not eat!

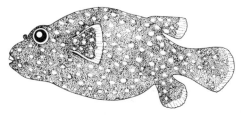

GUINEAFOWL and GOLDEN PUFFER, *Arothron meleagris.* **Bolete.** In
Cortez to Mulege. Inshore-onshore. Deep purple-black with small
white spots and white fin margins; there is also a solid golden
phase; puffs up like a ballon. Takes small baits; a pest at times.
Poor fighter. Some think this fish is **poisonous;** avoid eating.

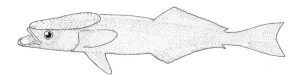

REMORA, Family Echeneididae. **Remora.** 6 or more species. Commonly
found throughout area attached to sharks, billfish, turtles, even
boats. Most are dark colored, all have characteristic sucker disc on
head. 8-12 in., to 30. Questionable food value.

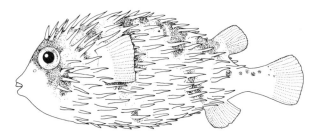

BALLOONFISH, *Diodon holocanthus.* **Pez erizo.** Magdalena to upper
Cortez. Inshore-onshore. Yellowish tan body with dark bars and
long, sharp spines; blows up like a balloon. To 18 inches. Takes
anything; a pest. Poor fighter. Some think this fish is **poisonous;**
avoid eating.

When Are They There?

In the approximately 12 degrees of latitude covered in the ten Baja Fishing Zones, there are varying temperature and current conditions. These, and other forces, keep a sizeable variety of fish moving, eating and being eaten at all times of the year. Sometimes wide areas, covering a number of fishing zones, erupt at once; at other times of the year, their activity concentrates in only one spot. The trick is to figure out where and when.

In the accompanying Baja Angling Calendars, the angler will find the answer as to location for the best fishing in each month. In order to help tell when, and where, the calendars have been tailored to each Baja Fishing Zone.

I would be foolish to say that what follows is 100% accurate—fish just don't operate that way. Never have I encountered such a perverse group of creatures when it comes to predicting what they are going to do; but nearly 30 years of personal fishwatching and hundreds—maybe thousands—of reports from others have gone into what is in this book. To illustrate my point, here are a few abnormal occurrences which took place in the Loreto area during the past few years.

It is traditional that dorado are literally jumping into the Loreto swimming pools on the Fourth of July, but in 1978 they didn't appear until well into August. Another year, the dorado stayed around all winter. Again in 1978, early summer saw a flurry of action on black marlin weighing less than 100 pounds; nobody had ever heard of such a thing. Three years earlier, the yellowtail came in with a bang on schedule in late November, only to disappear in December and not return until March; then they stuck around into June.

There are stories of a similar nature in every part of Baja. Fortunately, they are exceptions, but a novice angler visiting Baja for the first time could well come away with the belief that Tom Miller doesn't know what he is talking about. So at your own risk, and mine, read on.

ZONE I	J	F	M	A	M	J	J	A	S	O	N	D
Albacore												
Bass, Kelp												
Barracuda												
Bonito												
Croakers												
Dorado												
Marlin												
Perch, Barred												
Rock Cod												
Skipjack												
Swordfish												
Tuna, Bluefin												
Tuna, Yellowfin												
White Seabass												
Yellowtail												

NORTH PACIFIC

Ensenada's photographers kept busy in the late 50's taking pictures such as this of Elizabeth and Julian Garrett with yellowtail and bonito.

CENTRAL PACIFIC

ZONE II	J	F	M	A	M	J	J	A	S	O	N	D
Bonito	░	░	░	░	░	░	░	░	░	░	░	░
Cabrilla	░	░	░	░	░	█	█	█	█	█	░	░
Corvina	█	█	█	░	░	░	░	░	░	░	█	█
Croakers	░	░	░	░	█	█	█	█	█	█	░	░
Dorado	░	░	░	░	░	█	█	█	█	█	░	░
Giant Sea Bass	░	░	░	░	█	█	█	█	█	█	░	░
Groupers	░	░	░	░	░	░	░	░	░	░	░	░
Halibut	░	░	█	█	█	█	░	░	░	░	░	░
Skipjack								░	░	░	░	░
Tuna, Yellowfin	░	░	░	░	░	█	█	█	█	█	█	█
Wahoo	░	░	░				░	░	░	░	░	░
White Seabass	░	░	░	░	░	░						░
Yellowtail	█	█	█	█	█	█	█	█	█	█	█	█

Larry Funder, above, and Horace Brinton began fishing the beaches below Ensenada in the late 20's for croaker and corbina.

The moment of truth to see if that first marlin is a record fish.

MAGDALENA

ZONE III	J	F	M	A	M	J	J	A	S	O	N	D
Black Snook												
Bonito												
Cabrilla												
Corvinas												
Dorado												
Giant Sea Bass												
Groupers												
Halibut												
Sierra												
Snappers												
Tuna, Yellowfin												
Wahoo												
Yellowtail												

**C
A
B
O**

ZONE IV	J	F	M	A	M	J	J	A	S	O	N	D
Amberjack												
Bonito												
Cabrilla												
Dorado												
Groupers												
Jack Cravalle												
Marlin, Blue												
Marlin, Striped												
Roosterfish												
Sailfish												
Sierra												
Snappers												
Swordfish												
Tuna, Yellowfin												
Wahoo												
Yellowtail												

These three muchachos found a way to handle a 40 pound dorado without dragging it home in the sand.

TOM MILLER

TOM MILLER

Ten days on a Baja beach with jack cravalle and cabrilla left Frank Merrill of Lake Tahoe wondering what he ever saw in trout fishing.

E A S T   C A P E

ZONE V	J	F	M	A	M	J	J	A	S	O	N	D
Amberjack												
Bonito												
Cabrilla												
Dorado												
Groupers												
Jack Cravalle												
Marlin, Black												
Marlin, Blue												
Marlin, Striped												
Needlefish												
Pompano												
Roosterfish												
Sailfish												
Sierra												
Snappers												
Tuna, Yellowfin												
Wahoo												
Yellowtail												

L A P A Z

ZONE VI	J	F	M	A	M	J	J	A	S	O	N	D
Amberjack					░	░	░	░	░	░	░	
Bonito	░	░	░	░	░	░	░	░	░	░	░	░
Cabrilla	░	░	░	░	█	█	█	█	█	█	█	░
Dorado				░	░	█	█	█	█	█	░	
Groupers	░	░	░	░	█	█	█	█	█	█	█	░
Jack Cravalle				░	░	█	█	█	█	░	░	
Marlin, Black							░	░	░	░	░	
Marlin, Blue							░	░	░	░	░	
Marlin, Striped				░	░				░	░	░	
Needlefish	░	░	░	░	░	░	░	░	░	░	░	░
Pompano												
Roosterfish	░				░	░	░	░	░	░	░	
Sailfish					░	░	█	█	█	░	░	
Sierra	░	░	░	░	░	░	░	░	░	░	░	░
Snappers	░	░	░	█	█	█	█	█	█	█	░	░
Tuna, Yellowfin					░	░	█	█	█	█	█	░
Yellowtail	█	█	█	█	░	░	░					░

The roosterfish combines beauty, acrobatics, strength and a wiley nature to be one of the most exciting fish in the Cortez.

BILL BEEBE

TOM MILLER

Cabrilla may be taken from many beaches along the Cortez coast of Baja, and make excellent eating.

ZONE VII	J	F	M	A	M	J	J	A	S	O	N	D
Bonito			▒	▒	▒	▒	▒	▒	▒	▒		
Cabrilla		▒	█	█	█	█	█	█	█	█	█	▒
Dorado				▒	█	█	█	█	█	█	▒	
Giant Sea Bass			▒	▒	▒	▒						
Groupers		▒	█	█	█	█	█	█	█	█	█	▒
Jack Cravalle					▒	▒	▒	▒	▒	▒		
Marlin, Blue							▒	▒	▒	▒		
Marlin, Striped					▒	▒	▒	▒	▒			
Needlefish				▒	▒	▒	▒	▒	▒	▒	▒	
Pompano				▒	▒	▒	▒	▒	▒	▒		
Roosterfish			▒	▒	▒			▒	▒	▒	▒	
Sailfish						▒	▒	▒	▒	▒		
Sierra	█	█	█	▒	▒	▒	▒	▒	▒	▒	█	█
Snappers	▒	▒	▒	▒	█	█	█	█	█	█	▒	
Tuna, Yellowfin					▒	█	█	█	█	█	▒	
Yellowtail	█	█	█	▒	▒	▒					▒	▒

CORTEZ MIDRIFF

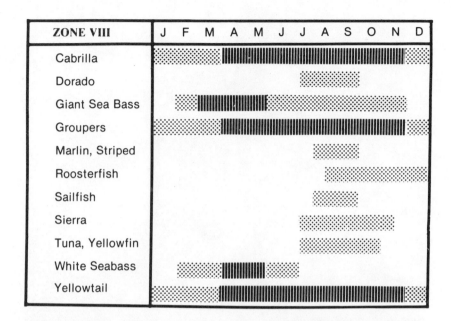

ZONE VIII	J	F	M	A	M	J	J	A	S	O	N	D
Cabrilla	░	░	░	█	█	█	█	█	█	█	█	░
Dorado							░	░	░			
Giant Sea Bass		░	█	█	█	░	░	░	░	░		
Groupers	░	░	░	█	█	█	█	█	█	█	█	░
Marlin, Striped							░	░	░			
Roosterfish								░	░	░		
Sailfish							░	░	░			
Sierra							░	░	░	░		
Tuna, Yellowfin							░	░	░	░		
White Seabass		░	░	█	█	░	░					
Yellowtail	░	█	█	█	█	█	█	█	█	█	█	░

The capture of a striped marlin is the goal of most anglers; the photo above is the dream of all photographers.

N O R T H   C O R T E Z

DWIGHT SHERRILL

In 1955, James Sherrill took two of these totuava while fishing with his dad at San Felipe. Not bad for a ten-year old.

ZONE IX	J	F	M	A	M	J	J	A	S	O	N	D
Cabrilla												
Corvinas												
Croakers												
Groupers												
Pompano												
Sierra												
White Seabass												
Yellowtail												

R E V I L L A G I G E D O S

ZONE X	J	F	M	A	M	J	J	A	S	O	N	D
Amberjack												
Cabrilla												
Dorado												
Groupers												
Marlin, Striped												
Marlin, Blue												
Snappers												
Tuna, Yellowfin												
Wahoo												

HURRICANE SEASON

TOM MILLER

A lineup across the stern of the yellowfin tuna over 150 pounds is a tradition for the long range boats visiting the Revillagigedo Islands.

Needlefish

For some years the most exasperating fish in the Cortez for me was the needlefish. I could see this long, slim and speedy creature following and slashing at my jigs as I trolled or retrieved over the shallow reefs of the lower Sea of Cortez, but getting one to the boat was a minor miracle. Because of their long, bony beak, the damn things were rarely hooked; when they were, their acrobatic "snap S double flip," which was performed as much as four feet above the water, almost assured a disconnect.

Finally, I came across a young Mexican boy who, with a handline and a beat up looking feather, was taking one four-footer after another. His success ratio was ten times mine! After five fish, I hustled over to watch.

The solution was so simple that I felt silly. On the shank of the hook portion of the jig he had firmly attached about ten loops of monofilament line. The loops acted as a snare to tangle with the needlefish's beak and many sharp teeth. Now, when I find a school of needlefish, I can have any number of exciting battles, appreciate their heroic jumps and still release the fish, but at my choice.

Man With A Plan

In September of 1978, a Mr. Shiro Saegusa from Japan walked into the office of Gordon Prentice of Baja Fishing Adventures and announced, through an interpreter, that he was going to La Paz to catch a very large marlin so that he might have it mounted for his home in Japan.

Prentice explained that at this particular time of the year few marlin of any kind were being taken around La Paz and suggested that he might be better off trying the area of Cabo San Lucas or the East Cape. Saegusa listened politely and nodded as the interpreter translated. No, he wished to go to La Paz; he had a brochure which said that there were marlin there and he held it out, the cover showing a huge billfish.

The gentleman was adamant; so against his better judgment, Prentice wrote up the trip. With smiles of satisfaction, the pair bowed and departed.

A week later the phone rang and it was his Japanese friends. They announced that everything had gone according to plan. Mr. Saegusa had indeed taken a trophy of sufficient size to meet his needs and he wished to express his appreciation. The trophy? A 318 pound striped marlin—the only marlin taken that week in La Paz and one of the largest to be taken in the Sea of Cortez! Truly, a man with a plan.

Supplemental Reading

Miller, Tom and Hoffman, Carol, **The Baja Book III,** Baja Trail Publications, Inc., Box 6088, Huntington Beach, CA 92615. $11.95 plus $.72 tax & $1.50 shipping. Baja's most popular roadguide series (142,000 copies in print) has been remapped, rewritten and updated. Exclusive "you are there" roadlogs tell, within meters, where you are on Baja's highways. Visit with the authors the latest resorts, trailer parks, marinas and airports. Fish, camp, beachcomb, windsail, surf and relax with those who know Baja best.

Miller, Tom, **Eating Your Way Through Baja.** Baja Trail Publications. 1986. $4.95 plus $.30 tax & $1.50 shipping. A lighthearted invitation to step beyond the conventional tourist hotel dining room and join the local Baja people at that special restaurant or taco stand where they eat. Laze in the shade of a palapa and feel the warmth of the people who live there. Eat your way through Baja with Tom Miller and enjoy every bite.

Miller, Shirley, **Mexico West Cookbook.** Baja Trail Publications. 1983. $4.95 plus $.30 tax & $1.50 shipping. A unique book adapting American recipes to what is available in Mexican markets, and Mexican recipes to American supermarket supplies. Brightly edited, whimsically illustrated.

Patchen, Marvln and Aletha, **Baja Adventures by Land, Air and Sea.** Baja Trail Publications. 1981. $9.95 plus $.60 tax & $1.50 shipping. Adventure comes in many forms in Baja California and the Patchens proved that one's imagination was the only limitation. Only some of the ways the Patchens have traveled Baja are: jeep, dunebuggy, canoe, helicopter and airplane, with hiking and diving thrown in. Fun reading with lots of valuable tips.

McMahon, Mike, **Adventures in Baja,** McMahon Press, Los Angeles, CA. 1983. An enteratining and somewhat irreverent look at Baja by a man who obviously has loved every minute of the more than 40 years he has spent in Baja.

Hunter, Ben, **The Baja Feeling,** Baja Trail Publications. 1976. $7.95 plus $1.50 shipping & tax. A classic narrative of love for the land, the people and the feeling. Well written. One you will have trouble putting down.

Cannon, Ray, **The Sea of Cortez.** Lane Publishing Co., Menlo Park, CA. 1966. So well did this beautiful 4-color book present the romance, the people and the fishing, that it became the subject of several TV features. Yes, this is the book that brought the angler, the yachtsman, and ultimately the investors to Baja. It supplied the excitement and the pizzaz to the Baja story, and still does if you can find a copy. Prices for a first edition are now topping $100.

Fishing Spanish

Several years ago an old friend and long time resident of Baja, Jerry Klink, wrote an article for *Salt Water Sportsman* magazine. In it he listed a number of words and phrases in Spanish, which, if learned, will cut through almost any language barrier which might exist between the fisherman and his Mexican crew.

First, a quick lesson in pronunciation. Spanish is an almost phonetic language. With few exceptions, the consonants are pronounced as in English. The pronunciation of the exceptions as well as the vowels is given below:

A—as the **a** in father
E—as the **e** in they
I—as the **i** in machine
O—as the **o** in over
U—as the **u** in rude
Y—as the **y** in yes
G—with **i** or **e**, as the **h** in home
G—with **a**, **o**, or **u** as the **g** in go
H—always silent
LL—as the **y** in yes
N—as the **ny** in canyon
Q—as the **c** in come
RR—has a double-triple-quadruple trill. Let your tongue rrrroll.
V—as **b**, or a combination of **b** and **v**

Almost all words have the accent on the next to the last syllable.

Now, let's have a look at Klink's fishing Spanish:

What is your name—**Cual es su nombre**
My name is—**Mi nombre es**
Stop—**Alto**
Go ahead—**Adelante**
Back up—**Para atrás**
Return to same spot—**Vamos al mismo lugar**
Turn left—**A la izquierda**
Turn right—**A la derecha**
Troll a little faster—**Poco mas rápido**
Troll a little slower—**Poco mas despacio**
Let's go—**Vamanos**
Just a second—**Un momento**
Hurry up—**Apúrate**
Bring in the line—**Enrolla la linea**
Change the bait—**Cambie la carnada**

I would like to fish for . . . —**Quiero pescar**
Let's fish for something else—**Quiero pescar algo diferente**
I want to fish near shore—**Quiero pescar en la orilla**
I want to fish out deep—**Quiero pescar en la hondo**
What kind of fish are here—**Que classe de pescado aqúi**
Let's anchor—**Tira el ancla**
Stop, I want to cast—**Alto, quiero casteár**
How deep is it here—**Que tan hondo aqui**
What is the best fishing at this time—**Que estan pescando ahora**
I want to set my own hook—**Yo quiero anzuelear**
Don't touch the line—**No tiente la linea**
Don't touch the rod—**No tiente la caña**
Boat the fish—**Enganchalo**
Release the fish—**Déjelo ir**
Tag the fish and release—**Márcalo y sueltalo**
What kind of fish is it—**Que classe de pescado**
How much does it weigh—**Quanto pesa**
    (a kilo is 2.2 pounds)
Is it good eating—**Se come**
I would like lunch—**Quiero lonchar**
I would like a soda—**Quiero refresco**
I would like a beer—**Quiero cerveza**
What place is that (pointing)—**Que lugar es ese**
Where is the head—**Donde esta el baño**
Let's go home—**Vamanos a la casa**
How much do I owe—**Cuanto de debo**
Keep it wet down, it may be a record—
    Mojalo, posible un record

Water—**Agua**
Boat—**Lancha**
Oars—**Remos**
Outriggers—**Tangones**
Engine—**Motór**
Bow—**Proa**
Stern—**Popa**
Reel—**Carrete**
Rod—**Caña**
Line—**Linea**
Swivel—**Destorcedór**
Leader—**Empate**
Hook—**Anzuelo**
Knot—**Nudo**
Bigger hook—**Anzuelo mas grande**
Smaller hook—**Anzuelo mas chico**
Feather—**Pluma**

Artificial lure—**Curricán**
Cut bait—**Pedazo de carnada**
Live bait—**Carnada viva**
Flying fish—**Voladór**
Sardines—**Sardinas**
Mullet—**Lisa**
Gaff—**Gancho**
Rocks—**Rocas**
Shore—**Orilla**
Island—**Isla**
South—**Sur**
North—**Norte**
I—**Yo**
You—**Usted**
Good—**Bueno**
Bad—**Malo**

Resorts

When getting ready to make that trip into Baja's prime fishing areas, it is advisable — almost mandatory in some instances — to make reservations in advance. A "plan ahead" mode is certainly a requirement over holiday times, such as Easter Week, Memorial Day, Fourth of July, Thanksgiving and the week between Christmas and New Year.

Although more visitors come camping to Baja each year, there are have been but few new trailer parks built during that same time frame, and most do not accept reservations. With that in mind we will recommend only a few in areas where it could get crowded and there is a chance of obtaining a reservation.

For the tent and offroad camper there are hundreds of beaches ot choose from. Just set up camp and stay about as long as you like. Some are just off the highway, near towns such as Mulege, Loreto and San Felipe, while others may be from five to fifty miles from anything.

We are making no effort to list all of hotels, etc. in Baja's fishing areas, instead we refer you to *The Baja Book III* (see Supplemental Reading). Write to addresses shown for more information.

ENSENADA
Cortez Motor Hotelthere , Box 396, Ensenada, B.C., Mexico.
Ensenada TraveLodge, Ave Bancarte 130, Ensenada, B.C. Mexico.
San Nicolas Hotel, Box 19, Ensenada, B.C. Mexico.
Hotel La Pinta, 3838 N. Belt East, No. 280, Houston, TX 77032.
Villa Marina, P.O. Box 28, Ensenada, B.C., Mexico.

SAN FELIPE
El Capitan Motel, Box 1916, Calexico, CA 92231.
Motel Villa del Mar, Av. Mar Baltico, San Felipe, B.C., Mexico.
Hotel Castel San Felipe, 664 Broadway, No. G, Chula Vista, CA 92010.
Hotel Riviera, Box 102, San Felipe, B.C., Mexico.
El Cortez Motel, Box 1227, Calexico, CA 92231.

SAN QUINTIN
Molino Viejo Motel Box 90, Valle de San Quintin, B.C., Mexico.

BAHIA DE LOS ANGELES
Casa Diaz Resort, P.O. Box 579, Ensenada, B.C., Mexico.
Villa Vitta Motel, 2904 Pacific Hwy., San Diego, CA 92101.

PUNTA CHIVATO
Hotel Punta Chivato, Box 18, Mulege, B.C.Sur, Mexico.

MULEGE
Hotel Las Casitas, Madero 50, Mulege, B.C.Sur, Mexico.
Hotel Vista Hermosa, 4440 Cattle Dr., Redding, CA 96003.
Hotel Serenidad, Box 9, Mulege, B.C.Sur, Mexico.

LORETO
Hotel La Pinta, Box 28, Loreto, B.C.Sur, Mexico.
Hotel Oasis, Box 17, Loreto, B.C.Sur, Mexico.

Resorts

Hotel Mision Loreto, Box 49, Loreto, B.C.Sur, Mexico.
El Presidente Loreto, 3838 N. Belt East, Houston, TX 77032.

LA PAZ
Hotel Los Arcos, 4332 Katella Ave., Los Alamitos, CA 90720.
La Posada, Box 152, La Paz, B.C.Sur, Mexico.
El Presidente La Paz, 3838 N. Belt East, No. 280, Houston, TX 77032.
Gran Baja Hotel, Box 223, La Paz, B.C.Sur, Mexico.

LOS PLANES
Hotel Las Arenas, Box 3766, Santa Fe Springs, CA 90670.

EAST CAPE
Punta Pescadero, Box 1044, Los Altos, CA 94023.
Playa Hermosa, Box 1827, Monterey, CA 93942.
Palmas de Cortez, Box 1284, Canoga Park, CA 91304.
Rancho Buena Vista, Box 673, Monrovia, CA 91016.
Spa Buena Vista, Box 2573, Canoga Park, CA 91306.
Punta Colorada, Box 1284, Canoga Park, 91304.

SAN JOSE DEL CABO
El Presidente Cabos, 3838 N. Belt East No. 280, Houston, TX 77032.
Hotel Castel Cabo, Box 8193, Chula Vista, CA 92012.
Hotel Calinda Aquamarina, Box 3009, Silver Springs, MD 20901
Hotel Palmilla, 4577 Viewridge Ave., San Diego, CA 92123.

CABO SAN LUCAS
Hotel Cabo San Lucas, Box 48088, Los Angeles, CA 90048.
Hotel Twin Dolphin, 1625 W. Olympic Blvd., Los Angeles, CA 90015.
Hotel Calinda Cabo Baja, Box 3009, Silver Springs, MD 20901.
Hacienda Beach Resort, Box 48872, Los Angeles, CA 90048.
Hotel Solmar, Box 383, Pacific Palisades, CA 90272.
Hotel Finisterra, 4332 Katella Ave., Los Alamitos, CA 90720.
Hotel Mar de Cortez, Box 1827, Monterey, CA 93942.

Special Trips

There are a variety of special fishing trips into Baja waters. The few below should whet your appetite. For more look on pages 142-6 in The Baja Book III.

Fisherman's Landing, 2838 Garrison St., San Diego, CA 92106
H & M Landing, 2803 Emerson, San Diego, CA 92106
Lee Palm Sportfishers, 2801 Emerson, San Diego, CA 92106
Point Loma Sportfishing Assn., 1403 Scott, San Diego, CA 92106
Tony Reyes Fishing Tours, 4010 E. Chapman ½D, Orange, CA 92669
La Paz Fishing, PO Box 764, Crestline, CA 92325
Jig Stop Tours, 34186 Coast Hwy, Dana Point, CA 92629
Ramona Castro & Sons, Box 974, Ensenada, B.C., Mexico
Baja Adventures, 16000 Ventura Blvd, No.200, Encino, CA 91436
Baja Safari, Box 1827, Monterey, CA 93942

A World of Records

Who among us has never yearned to leave our mark in the fishing world by taking a record-size fish? At least once in our lives we all would like to take that one fish which would be recognized by the world as a great accomplishment. And there is probably no single area of the world where there are more opportunities to set a new world record than in the seas around the Baja Califorina peninsula.

According to the International Game Fish Association, at least 34 species that they currently recognize for world records are found in Baja waters. In addition an all-tackle category not restricted to certain species includes any sport fish caught on rod and reel in accordance with IGFA rules. Thus there are hundreds of opportunities to put your name in the record book, to remain until someone comes along and catches a bigger one. Why not give it a try.

Line and tackle categories are — in kilograms and (pounds): 1(2), 2(4), 4(8), 6(12), 8(16), 10(20), 15(30), 24(50), 37(80) and 60(130) in both mens' and ladies' divisions for conventional or spinning. For fly fishermen the categories are: 1(2), 2(4), 4(8), 6(12) and 8(16) test leaders, again in kilos and (pounds).

A letter to the IGFA, 3000 East Las Olas Blvd., Fort Lauderdale, FL 33316-1616 USA, will get you complete information on rules, entry blanks, etc. Their monthly bulletins and fine annual publilcation, World Record Marine Fishes, are well worth the modest membership fee of $25.

TOM MILLER

Though Dawn Porter's small blue marlin was not a world record, it was a personal best on light line.

Mexico Fishing Regulations

Permits to fish or sport dive from a commercial passenger-carrying sportboat in Mexican waters is usually included in the price of the trip. However, anyone 16 or older fishing or diving off a private boat or from the shore, must have a standard Mexican fishing license.

A licensed angler may catch a total of 10 fish per day — and no more than five of one species — but only two roosterfish or doardo (dolphinfish), one marlin, sailfish, swordfish or black sea bass. Fish that are released are not included in the count. Nearly all of the Baja resorts strongly encourage that healthy billfish be released, thus conserving the resource.

Visiting anglers usually hold within the stipulated limits, but those few who do not do a great disservice to all who observe the intent of the law. The whole idea of the regulations is for the sportsman not to take more than can be reasonably used or stored safely. Canning of large amounts of fish is forbidden. The only problems we've seen have been when over-zealous fishermen have taken more than they can use, or their ice chest can store.

Possession of cabrilla, lobster, abalone, oysters, pismo clams or shrimp is forbidden, though you probably will not be challenged if you have a small amount for "immediate personal consumption," as long as it is not during a closed season, and you have a valid fishing license. Possession of a totuava is now permitted under certain circumstances, you may not bring any part of the fish into the United States as our government considers them an endangered species.

Permits are available through the Mexio West Travel Club, 2424 Newport Blvd. Suite T91, Costa Mesa CA 92627; a number of tackle stores near the border (including some in the Los Angeles area; and at

TOM MILLER

The future of fishing in Baja will depend greatly on the preservation of species such as this black snook, and in the education of these young men to the fact that their future is inexorably linked to the decisions and practices of their fathers.

the Mexican Department of Fisheries in San Diego. They may also be purchased at fisheries offices in Mexico, but supplies are spotty. Prices vary as the value of the peso fluctuates, but are less expensive than a California state fishing license.

A Resource-Full Sea

Historically, the seas surrounding the Baja California peninsula have been rich ones. The coves and the esteros abounded with plankton, clams, oysters and a myriad of other invertebrates which were the beginnings of the bounty of life poured out into the sea taking their place in the order of things. It is an eat-and-be-eaten world. When left to their own devices, the cycles repeated themselves, millenia after millenia, but now man has stepped into the picture.

Those of us who have spent years participating in the Baja experience began noticing the difference within the past few years. It was the same scenario played out over the past few decades here in the United States.

Large ships spread huge nets to gather whatever they could find to feed the steam-belching canneries and reduction plants in some distant port. Near shore, productive reefs became unapproachable because of the dozens of gill nets set by the men living in tiny fish camps. Divers took advantage of calm seas to harvest abalone; well-baited traps drew lobsters and crabs toward their final destination—the freezer locker in an American restaurant or supermarket—and the esteros began to loose their abundance of shellfish.

Today, the harvesting continues in Mexico as it does in the United States, certainly at a faster pace than is safe for the marine stocks. But there are some lights appearing on both sides of the border which, when joined together, may produce a series of clear and well-defined regulations upon which will depend the continued rich resources of the west coast of Mexico and the United States.

More and more resorts are encouraging the policy of catch and release of billfish. Most fishing tournaments held in Baja now offer bonus points for released fish, and the anglers themselves are enthusiastically joining in the effort. This was well illustrated by a group who fished out of Rancho Buena Vista in the summer of 1978.

None of the party of eight had ever taken a marlin or sail but they agreed to tag and release all fish. By the end of the week, all had taken at least one big fish and they could look proudly toward a count of 19 billfish tagged and released—but they had no pictures. On the last day another fisherman brought in a badly hooked marlin that had no chance to survive. Before the huge fish was cut up for food, all eight posed with "their" fish. Now they had pictures to show at home, plus the good feeling of knowing that 19 marlin and sailfish were still free to live.

As a close observer of the Baja fishing scene, I have learned of several bi-national research studies which, it is hoped, will lead to additional international agreements and contribute to a growing knowledge at all levels for the maintenance of a healthy balance between commercial and sport fishing.

Huachinango Express

It would not be considered correct to complete a book on fishing without including at least one fish-eating story. This one is about the red snapper, or huachinango.

During our years of travel along Mexico's coastal stretches my ex-wife was always on the lookout for a restaurant with "Huachinango Frito" on the menu. From Guaymas to the Guatamala border, around Merida, Cancun or Veracruz, and from Mulege to the Cape, her antenna was tuned to any sign — sensory or visual — of the existence of a huachinango. A sometimes-enthusiastic fisherman, she often stayed ashore to read, but always with the admonition that at least one red snapper be included in the catch.

The huachinango is best when it weighs no more than two pounds, when it can be prepared whole. To cook . . . Gill, gut and thoroughly scale. If necessary to get it into the pan, remove head and tail. With a knife, cut through the skin almost to the backbone in two or three places on each side, alternating so they do not connect. Sprinkle with seasoned flour and deep-fry in hot lard seasoned with a dozen or so chopped garlic cloves. Serve with fresh lime. WOW!

More fish-fix'n recipes are found in *THE BAJA BOOK III* and the *MEXICO WEST COOKBOOK*. See reading list on page 118.

TOM MILLER

Whether on the beach or in the finest of restaurants, the Mexican huachinango frito will stand out as a special experience.